America Looks West

Lewis and Clark on the Missouri

NEBRASKAland Maga

Volume 80, Number 7, August-September 200

Published monthly except for combined January-February and August-September issu
the Nebraska Game and Parks Commission, 2200 N. 33rd Street, Lincoln, NE 68503.

ISSN: 0028-1964
Periodicals postage paid at Lincoln, Nebraska.
POSTMASTER: Send all address changes to NEBRASKAland Magazine,
P.O. Box 30370, Lincoln, NE 68503-0370.

Cover: Silhouetted by the setting sun, a replica keelboat and pirogues, used in the filming of the large-format movie *Lewis and Clark: Great Journey West,* ply the Missouri River near Niobrara, Nebraska. Photo by Eric Fowler.

Inside Front Cover: A stretch of the Missouri, near Niobrara, Nebraska, resembles the natural river with backwater sloughs and marshes alongside the serpentine main channel. Photo by Eric Fowler.

Above: Portraits of Meriwether Lewis (left) and William Clark painted by Charles Willson Peale.

Contents

MISSOURI HISTORICAL SOCIETY, ST. LOUIS / PHOTO BY DAVID SCHULTZ

Meriwether Lewis's watch and telescope rest with William Clark's compass atop their red-leather bound journals. The 28-month, 8,000-mile Expedition from St. Louis to the Oregon Pacific coast and back in 1804-1806 is the epic American journey. An arduous adventure known for scientific discoveries, the Corps of Discovery established the United States' claim on the West and began its subjugation of Indians.

Introduction

IN THE SPRING OF 1804, when a handful of U.S. soldiers started up the muddy Missouri River in a 55-foot keelboat and two smaller craft, the world took little notice. Only a few Americans living across the Mississippi from St. Louis in the frontier settlement of Goshen, Illinois, were around to see them. Information traveled slowly, no faster than a ship, boat or man on horseback, so all news was delayed, and few beyond Goshen or St. Louis would hear of the departure any time soon.

Today, however, as the nation commemorates the bicentennial of that Voyage of Discovery, virtually anything connected with the Lewis and Clark Expedition attracts a great deal of attention. Books have been written, films made and documentaries aired. Living historians have perfected their characters and communities have planned events. And the National Park Service, through its Lewis and Clark National Historic Trail and with the help of various other organizations, encourages and supports these efforts. Two centuries after the fact, the Lewis and Clark Expedition is big news.

As the green troops on those boats in 1804 labored through what is now Missouri, Kansas, Iowa and Nebraska, they became more seasoned each day, and they soldiered like veterans through South Dakota, North Dakota and beyond. Of course, those place names were meaningless then, but as we commemorate the explorers' efforts 200 years later, there's a temptation to divide the story into these little close-to-home segments. This story suffers, however, when told piecemeal. This issue presents the account of the entire Expedition, emphasizing the first year and the Missouri River.

Lewis and Clark's exploration was a pivotal event in the nation's history, setting the stage for discovery, settlement and development of the West that proceeded at a breathtaking pace. By traversing and mapping the Columbia River, they strengthened the claim of the United States to the Oregon Territory.

The Expedition launched the fur trade in earnest with reports of a country filled with beaver. European nations traded with Indians for furs, but men from the states went west and did the trapping themselves. They entered uncharted areas, discovered mountain passes and helped map most of the West. In the 1840s, immigrants in wagons began following the routes established by the trappers and mountain men, and three decades later, railroads brought a flood of European immigrants to populate the Plains.

The remarkably rapid incorporation of this vast region into our country began with Lewis and Clark, and it is why we celebrate – or rather, why most of us celebrate. Others, descendants of those who lived in the West long before Lewis and Clark arrived, see things differently. They may not celebrate the Lewis and Clark bicentennial, but many will participate to provide another point of view, the American Indian versions of the story. Regardless of personal perspective, the Voyage of Discovery is a fascinating story and a watershed event in American history, the young nation's first bold step across the vast continent that it would one day span.

When Meriwether Lewis left the nation's capital in 1803, he carried the best map of North America then available (see pages 94-95). It was virtually blank from the Mississippi River to the Pacific Coast and the empty space was marked in large letters "conjectural." By 1890, the territory represented by this blank spot had become so fenced, farmed and filled with people that the historian Frederick Jackson Turner declared the American frontier at an end. The period of exploration, settlement and mass-migration, which had its beginnings with Lewis and Clark, lasted less than 90 years, but influences our culture to this day.

– Ken Bouc

Exploring the Missouri River to its source, the Corps of Discovery left St. Louis in May 1804 and returned in September 1806. In between the explorers traveled west (red line), wintering in 1804-1805 at Fort Mandan. They reached the Pacific Ocean in late-1805 and spent that winter at Fort Clatsop before turning east (blue line), and dividing the party to explore areas of what is now Montana on the return trip.

Poised for Discovery

By Harry W. Fritz

Jefferson's vision of westward expansion and Napoleon's decision to sell all the Louisiana territory was a happy coincidence. Jefferson's "Voyage of Discovery" would explore U.S. territory after all.

IT IS IMPOSSIBLE TO KNOW the precise moment when Thomas Jefferson, President of the United States, decided to send a military expedition up the Missouri River in search of a waterway to the West, but it happened sometime late in 1802. Nor is it possible to sort out with quantitative precision the many influences that impelled Jefferson's decision. His whole life pointed in that direction.

Jefferson was born on April 13, 1743, on what was then the western edge of settlement in Virginia. From his father and others he had heard tales about the lands beyond the Blue Ridge, and about the headwaters of the Ohio River, although he never set out to see them for himself. When Jefferson traveled, he headed east to Williamsburg, to Philadelphia, to France and Europe. The farthest west he ever ventured was a trip in 1818 to Warm Springs, about 60 miles west of Staunton, Virginia, and he couldn't wait to get home. He wrote his famous description of the confluence of the Potomac and Shenandoah rivers without having ever seen it. Other writers and explorers satisfied Jefferson's curiosity about the West. He imbibed their knowledge and recorded their discoveries, but he himself was an armchair geographer.

Jefferson's West was expansive. In *Notes on the State of Virginia,* his only book, published in 1787, we find him ascending the Missouri River and carefully calculating distances from Santa Fe, the capital of Spain's northern provinces. Jefferson believed, with Robert Rogers and other 18th century geographers, that all the great rivers of the West originated on the same plateau, or "height of land."

At the headwaters of the Missouri one would be within striking distance of the Columbia, the Rio Grande, the Colorado, Arkansas, and Platte rivers. Geopolitically and militarily, the power which controlled this pyramidal height of land would dominate the American West. The seed of the Lewis and Clark Expedition had been planted.

On three occasions before becoming president, Jefferson toyed with western exploration. In 1783, as a Confederation Congressman in Philadelphia, he wrote an old family friend, George Rogers Clark, the Virginia hero of the American

---

Harry W. Fritz has written several articles and lectured widely on the Lewis and Clark Expedition. He teaches at The University of Montana in Missoula, where he is chairman of the history department.

THOMAS JEFFERSON / CHARLES WILLSON PEALE

In 1802, President Thomas Jefferson decided to send an American expedition to explore the West.

Revolution in the West, asking him to explore the vast country between the Mississippi and California. Clark, who was broke, declined. Twenty years later Clark's brother William, 17 years George's junior, would receive a similar invitation from Meriwether Lewis.

In Paris in 1785, Jefferson met John Ledyard, a former Dartmouth student whose trip down the Connecticut River to Long Island Sound is replicated each year by the Ledyard Canoe Club. Ledyard had sailed with Captain James Cook in the 1770s to the northwest coast and the South Seas. Tattooed from head to toe, his head was filled with ideas of sea otters, trading posts, and western exploration. The closest he came, with Jefferson's help, was an overland trip through Russia to Irkutsk in Siberia, with the intention of crossing the Bering Sea and walking across America, west to east. But Tsarina Catherine had him arrested, so there are no counties named Ledyard in Nebraska.

André Michaux was a French botanist who resided and traveled in America between 1785 and 1796. In 1793, he interested Secretary of State Jefferson and the American Philosophical Society in Philadelphia in a proposed expedition to the Pacific. Jefferson raised some money and prepared instructions "to find the shortest & most convenient route of communication between the U.S. & the Pacific ocean" via the Missouri River. Michaux made it as far as Kentucky.

In these aborted endeavors Jefferson was not the chief initiator. He was ready to take advantage of the aspirations of others, but others appeared only sporadically. In 1802, however, Jefferson was president. The Northwest still beckoned. Ever since American ship captain Robert Gray had discovered the mouth of the Columbia River in 1792, a lucrative China trade in sea otter skins had attracted Spanish, English, and American merchants. Now economics, diplomacy, and exploration coincided.

Alexander Mackenzie worked for the British North West Company, trading for furs in the interior of the Canadian West. In 1789, he floated to the Arctic Ocean down the mighty river that bears his name. Three years later he became the first known European to cross the upper American continent, traveling down the Fraser River and overland to the Pacific Coast. His exploits remained unknown until he published *Voyages from Montreal* in 1801. Jefferson read Mackenzie's proposal to lock up the fur trade in the Columbia Basin by building forts and establishing connections to the East. The race was on.

The land tract known as Louisiana, which included all western drainages of the Mississippi River, had been claimed by France ever since the excursions of Marquette and Joliet in the late-17th century. The only French settlement in that vast area, and the only part of the territory east of the river, was New Orleans. In 1763, as part of the settlement ending the Seven Years War, Louisiana passed into Spanish hands. Spain therefore controlled the "right of deposit," the right of American farmers to float goods down the Mississippi and unload them in the city. This was a contentious issue between the United States and Spain, until resolved in

SALMONBERRY / FREDERICK PURSH (FLORA AMERICAE SEPTENTRIONALIS, PL. 16)

Lewis and Clark documented many plants unknown to science. One was the salmonberry *(Rubus spectabilis)* discovered in 1806 in the Columbia River Valley.

HERDS OF BISON AND ELK ON THE UPPER MISSOURI / KARL BODMER

America's favor by Pinckney's Treaty of 1796.

The world's diplomatic and power axis shifted dramatically on October 1, 1800, when, in the secret Treaty of San Ildefonso, Napoleonic France reacquired Louisiana from Spain. France never actually took control of Louisiana; Spanish authorities remained in charge. But, then as now, governments had trouble keeping secrets, and when President Jefferson heard rumors of the retrocession, he acted. "There is on the globe one single spot, the possessor of which is our natural and habitual enemy," he wrote to the U.S. Minister to France, Robert Livingston. "It is New Orleans." Jefferson did not fear a weak and "feeble" Spain, but France, the most powerful nation on Earth, must not be permitted to block American aspirations. Jefferson's fears became real in October, 1802, when Spanish authorities

The West was unknown to Jefferson and his countrymen in 1803 when the Lewis and Clark Expedition began its journey. The U.S. explorers marveled at the bounty of buffalo and elk along the upper Missouri River when they came upon scenes such as this one painted by Karl Bodmer 30 years later in what is now Montana.

BISON DANCE OF THE MANDAN INDIANS / KARL BODMER

One of Jefferson's missions for the explorers was to acquaint themselves with the Indian tribes and their customs, uses of agriculture, hunting and fishing, and their commerce. The Expedition spent the winter of 1804-1805 with the Mandan and Hidatsa tribes in present-day North Dakota. The Indians provided valuable information about the upper Missouri River. In 1834, artist Karl Bodmer observed a Buffalo Bull dance of Mandan men at Fort Clark and later re-created it in aquatint from his field drawings.

in New Orleans revoked the right of deposit.

Jefferson initiated three actions to weaken France's hold on Louisiana. First, he authorized Livingston in Paris to buy land on the lower Mississippi for use as a port, or to negotiate for free navigation and the right of deposit. Second, he wheedled $2 million from Congress, gave it to James Monroe, and sent him to France to buy New Orleans and West Florida. Third, he began to plan, this time on his own initiative, for an American expedition up the Missouri River, into the heart of Louisiana.

It is a telling fact that the first hard evidence of Jefferson's exploration plans is found in a letter from the Spanish Minister to America, Carlos Martinez de Yrujo, to his Minister of Foreign Affairs, Don Pedro Cevallos, dated December 2, 1802. Yrujo related a conversation he had had "the other day" with the President. Jefferson had inquired into the reaction of the Spanish government if "a group of travelers" were to "form a small caravan and go and explore the course of the Missouri River" with "no other view than the advancement of the geography." When Yrujo demurred, Jefferson elaborated: "Its object would not be other than

to observe the territories which are found between 40 degrees and 60 degrees from the mouth of the Missouri to the Pacific Ocean." Jefferson mentioned Mackenzie, and raised the possibility of a "continual communication, or little interrupted, by water as far as the South Sea."

Three points are significant here. First, the United States did not yet own Louisiana. What would become the Lewis and Clark Expedition was not initiated to explore American territory. Jefferson planned a commercial, literary, and geographical investigation of lands owned by France with the sufferance of Spain. Second, the President had no intention of stopping at the borders of Louisiana. He would proceed to the Pacific through territory claimed by Spain, Great Britain, and Russia. International consequences multiplied. Indeed, 60 degrees north latitude placed the limits of American ambition at the present border between British Columbia and the Yukon. Finally, Yrujo was on to Jefferson. He would "perpetuate the fame of his administration . . . by discovering or attempting at least to discover the way by which the Americans may someday extend their population and their influence up to the coasts of the South Sea."

Meriwether Lewis Prepares the Expedition

Enter Meriwether Lewis. The U.S. Army captain from Jefferson's neighborhood in Virginia had been working in the White House as the President's private secretary since April 1801. His job was not to file papers or take dictation, but to serve as a diplomatic courier and a military aide-de-camp. "Your knolege of the Western country, of the army and of all it's interests," Jefferson told Lewis, qualified him for the job. One of his first tasks was to grade the army officer corps according to its politics, so the President would know who his Republican friends were.

Lewis had not been employed to prepare for a western expedition. An organized venture up the Missouri River awaited future developments. Yet, by early-1803, Lewis was helping Jefferson calculate the costs of such a trip, and he was undoubtedly the "intelligent officer" Jefferson had in mind when he informed Congress on January 18 of his plans. There is no executive order naming Lewis commander, but on February 27, 1803, Jefferson revealed his name to Benjamin Smith Barton, a physician and naturalist.

Lewis spent the spring of 1803 preparing for the trip. He traveled to the federal armory at Harpers Ferry, Virginia, to order arms and the skeleton of a portable canoe. He took a crash course in celestial observation from the mathematician Andrew Ellicott in Lancaster, Pennsylvania. He headed to Philadelphia to study medicine with Benjamin Rush, botany with Barton, and zoology with Caspar Wistar. He pored over maps and journals, and gathered supplies and equipment. Most important, he invited his old friend and former commander, William Clark, to join him in the "fatiegues," dangers, and honors of an excursion to the Pacific. Clark signed on, and the rest is history.

Two weeks before Lewis departed Washington, Jefferson set down in writing his expectations of success. "The object of your mission," he stated bluntly, "is to explore the Missouri river, & such principal stream of it, as, by it's course and communication with the waters of the Pacific ocean, whether the Columbia, Oregan, Colorado or any other river may offer the most direct & practicable water communication across this continent for the purposes of commerce." The President wanted careful observations, measurements, and records. He was interested in Indians, animals, mineral potential, and climate. How close is the Missouri to the Rio Grande, and the Colorado? Can we horn in on the fur trade? Be careful, and come home safely.

Unknown to either Jefferson or Lewis, diplomats Monroe and Livingston took it upon themselves to sign a treaty on May 2, 1803, in Paris, and transferred the entire Louisiana territory, all 828,000 square miles of it, from France to the United States for the price of $15 million. All the pieces were now in place, for Jefferson, Lewis, Clark, and America.

A Corps of Discovery

By Bob Moore

Between the Nation's 27th and 28th birthdays, Lewis and Clark moved boats and supplies from Pittsburgh to a winter camp near St. Louis, recruited men and led them to the threshold of the Plains.

A STEADY DRIZZLE QUIETLY SOAKED THE MEN as they strained to load a final, heavy barrel onto the long wooden boat. Most of them wore military clothing and some were even wearing their brilliant blue and red regimental coats. Civilian well-wishers gathered nearby, having walked the three miles from the local settlement, Goshen, Illinois. Were they about to witness something historic? Only time would tell.

A tin horn was brought out by a sergeant, and an officer, dressed in his best uniform coat and cocked hat, ordered it blown. A long, low, mournful note signaled the soldiers on the bank of the Wood River to board the three boats tethered there, a stone's throw from the mighty Mississippi River. The men cast off lines, the crowd cheered, and the unpainted 55-foot keelboat and two smaller pirogues, one red and the other white, slipped off into the mist of the gray, wet afternoon. It was three o'clock on May 14, 1804, and Captain William Clark was leading his little flotilla westward toward a rendezvous with Meriwether Lewis and destiny.

The Lewis and Clark Expedition has been described as "the greatest camping trip of all time," a voyage of high adventure, and an exercise in manifest destiny, which carried the American flag overland to the Pacific Ocean. The Expedition was all of this and more. In fact, the story of the preparations for the journey, about how these men came to be at the Wood River in May 1804, is nearly as interesting as the story of their voyage.

The Expedition was the fulfillment of a long-held dream of President Thomas Jefferson. It would be accomplished by following the Missouri River to its source, then crossing the crest of the Rocky Mountains to find the headwaters of the Columbia. An easy pass through the mountains coupled with the close proximity of the headwaters of the Missouri and the Columbia might constitute the long-sought Northwest Passage across the continent. If the Americans found such a passage, they could corner lucrative trade with Asia.

In addition to finding the best route across the continent, the Expedition had two major goals. First, it was to be a diplomatic mission meant to contact American Indian nations in the Louisiana Purchase, establish the United States as sovereign

---

Bob Moore is the historian at the Jefferson National Expansion Memorial in St. Louis, Missouri. He has a master's degree from Washington University in St. Louis and is completing his doctorate. He is author of Native Americans: A Portrait.

THE DEPARTURE FROM THE WOOD RIVER ENCAMPMENT, MAY 14, 1804 / GARY R. LUCY

over the region and claim a major portion of the fur trade. Second, it was to be a voyage of scientific discovery, charged with describing and classifying all they would see on their route. Left unstated was a third goal, which was to stake a claim to the lands of the Pacific Northwest and provide for the eventual territorial expansion of the United States across the continent.

Jefferson's ambitions for the Expedition were large, and there were some very bold assumptions in his instructions. First, it was assumed that the Rockies were comparable to the Appalachians in height and difficulty of ascent, and second, that any stream to the west of the Rockies would naturally flow to the Columbia River drainage.

The Expedition began with the acquisition of supplies and the training of its appointed leader. Jefferson wrote letters of introduction for his 29-year-old personal secretary, Meriwether Lewis, to the most distinguished American scientists of the day, who prepared Lewis to explore, map and chronicle everything of interest, as Jefferson put it, along "the only line of easy communication across the continent."

On February 27, 1803, Jefferson confided in a letter to Benjamin Smith Barton, a physician and naturalist at the University of Pennsylvania, why he chose Lewis to head the Expedition. "It was impossible to find a character who to a compleat

With William Clark in command, on May 14, 1804, the Corps of Discovery left its Wood River training camp in a 55-foot keelboat and two smaller pirogues, one painted white and the other red. To propel the laden keelboat against the current while avoiding snags, the men used sails, oars and long poles. Sometimes the boats had to be pulled upriver with ropes by the men walking on the shore, a procedure called "cordelling." The grueling work moved the party 10 to 15 miles per day.

science in botany, natural history, mineralogy & astronomy, joined the firmness of constitution & character, prudence, habits adopted to the woods, & a familiarity with the Indian manners & character, requisite for this undertaking . . . Altho' no regular botanist he possesses a remarkable store of accurate observation on all the subjects of the three kingdoms, & will therefore readily single out whatever presents itself new to him in either."

On April 19, 1803, Lewis arrived in Lancaster, Pennsylvania, to learn to plot latitude and longitude from astronomer Andrew Ellicott. Lewis next traveled to Philadelphia where he met with Dr. Benjamin Rush, the most eminent American physician of his day, to learn about medicine. Lewis moved on to study with Dr. Barton, who instructed him in botany and zoology. Dr. Caspar Wistar rounded out Lewis' instruction in the natural sciences. A native of Philadelphia, and like

PLANNING THE EXPEDITION / LOUIS ARCHAMBAULT

In late-summer 1802, President Thomas Jefferson received a copy of a book by Alexander Mackenzie describing his 1793 trek across Canada in an attempt to find a passage for British trade to the Pacific. Jefferson chose his secretary, Meriwether Lewis, to lead a United States expedition across the West, and the two men met to plan the journey. Jefferson wrote a letter to Lewis outlining the purposes of the exploration: To find a Northwest Passage, to contact Indian tribes for future trade, and to conduct scientific investigations in the uncharted region.

BEYOND THE NEXT BEND / MARK S. RAITHEL

Rush and Barton schooled in Edinburgh, Scotland, Wistar taught anatomy at the University of Pennsylvania's medical school.

Lewis left Philadelphia on June 1 and traveled to Washington, D.C., to meet with Jefferson and make final arrangements for his journey to the Pacific. These included writing a long letter on June 19 to an old friend and former military commander, William Clark. Lewis asked Clark whether he would like to join the Expedition as its co-leader, and also requested that he recruit men for the Expedition.

Lewis left Washington on July 5, 1803, for Harpers Ferry, where he picked up the over 3,500 pounds of supplies and equipment he had amassed and paid to have it hauled overland to the Pittsburgh area. He was held up for over a month at Elizabeth, Pennsylvania, waiting for a 55-foot keelboat to be built.

The keelboat was finally completed on August 30 and Lewis began his journey down the Ohio River, bringing along a second, smaller, boat called a pirogue. The water was low, causing long portages and many delays that must have been vexing. Lewis made the first entry in the Expedition's official log that day, and while on the Ohio began to record scientific observations long before venturing into the uncharted country of the West.

Captains Lewis and Clark with Seaman, Lewis's Newfoundland dog, survey the Missouri River Valley in this depiction of a bluff in central Missouri. York, Clark's slave, gives his hand to another member of the party climbing the rocks. The Expedition's boats are beached on a sandbar in the river below.

That first journal entry chronicled an incident than nearly opened the Expedition on a tragic note. On a brief stop the afternoon of the first day, some residents of the area asked to see Lewis's airgun, which was made for him in Philadelphia. Lewis fired several shots as a demonstration. Then, while a spectator was examining the piece, it discharged accidentally, and a woman about 40 yards away fell, blood gushing from her temple. Fortunately, the ball had just grazed her and the wound was not serious.

Airguns of the day could be deadly and were definitely not toys. The 34-inch brass barrel of Lewis's piece fired .31 caliber lead balls with air compressed in the hollow butt stock reservoir at as much as 900 pounds per square inch. But airguns were not practical for serious use because of their high cost, and because they lacked the power that only a large caliber black powder firearm of the day could provide. Lewis's airgun, however, would prove useful at councils with Indians, who were greatly impressed with something that could shoot so accurately and quickly, and without the usual smoke, fire and noise.

Gathering Men and Equipment

On October 14, 1803, the keelboat arrived in Clarksville, Indiana, where Lewis joined William Clark, Clark's slave, York, and the men Clark had recruited. These so-called "nine young men from Kentucky" would form the backbone of the Expedition's crew. The party got under way once more on October 27, moving down the Ohio to Fort Massac, Illinois, where they met the half-Shawnee, half-French interpreter, George Drouillard. Lewis sensed that Drouillard was a real frontiersman with what we might today call "the right stuff," and hired him immediately. After studying the confluence of the Ohio and Mississippi rivers at Cairo, Illinois, they proceeded up the Mississippi, working against the current.

At Kaskaskia, Illinois, Lewis and Clark realized that their struggles with the Mississippi demonstrated the need for a larger detachment of men to move the supply-laden boats up the river. More manpower would also be needed when the Expedition got underway in the spring of 1804, to move the boats against the Missouri's muddy spring flood, prompting Lewis to "borrow" 12 soldiers from the Fort Kaskaskia's infantry and artillery regiments. The party also acquired a third boat, another pirogue, to carry the extra men and supplies. The boats were moved up the river to Cahokia, then one of the major towns in the Indiana Territory (today's State of Illinois) situated nearly opposite Spanish-held St. Louis.

Meriwether Lewis carried this ship's master-type telescope, with five brass and one wood-and-leather collapsible sections, to the Pacific Ocean and back. It was made by William Cary in London in about 1802.

MISSOURI HISTORICAL SOCIETY, ST. LOUIS / GLENN S. HENSLEY PHOTO

On December 8, 1803, Lewis traveled across the Mississippi River to St. Louis, then a town of just 925 residents, to meet with Lieutenant Governor Charles Dehault Delassus, a short, bespectacled Frenchman in the service of Spain. Through an interpreter, Lewis asked Delassus's permission to continue up the Missouri River. Delassus told Lewis in a genial fashion that he could not proceed without clearance from higher Spanish authorities, or until the official transfer of Upper Louisiana in the spring. Louisiana was still, officially, a foreign country.

Lewis rejoined Clark at Cahokia the following day. They decided that they would remain in the St. Louis area for the winter to stock up on supplies and gather information from fur traders and explorers.

Clark took the soldiers, recruits and the three boats up the Mississippi about 18 miles, putting in at the mouth of the River Dubois, today's Wood River, on the Illinois side. Looking out across the Mississippi, Clark could see the mouth of the Missouri River, which would be the departure point of the Expedition in the spring. Somewhere along the small stream Clark established "Camp River Dubois," Dubois being French for "Wood."

The area had plenty of timber, fresh water and game. It was a safe distance away from the allurements of a settlement, and was easily supplied via the river. A commissary of the regular U.S. Army provisioned the camp, and a woman was hired as a laundress and to mend clothing. Although some of the men were given passes to hunt for game, the camp depended for the most part on army pork, flour

MERIWETHER LEWIS / MICHAEL HAYNES

Meriwether Lewis was born in Virginia in 1774, and was 30 years old at the time of the Expedition's departure. He joined the army in 1794 and served in a special rifle company, where he was commanded by Lieutenant William Clark. A friendship developed that lasted until Lewis's death. When Thomas Jefferson was elected president in 1801, he asked Lewis to be his personal secretary and, later, to prepare to lead a journey of discovery to the Pacific Ocean. Lewis asked his old friend William Clark to be the co-commander of the Expedition. Lewis is often shown with a spontoon, a short pike carried by infantry officers in the 18th and early-19th centuries.

After the Expedition, Lewis settled in St. Louis and was appointed governor of the Louisiana Territory, but he seemed uneasy in that sedentary post. When the government refused to reimburse him for official expenditures in 1809, he started eastward to provide an explanation. He never made it to Washington. He died of a gunshot at a small inn along the Natchez Trace.

Jefferson and Clark felt certain that Lewis had committed suicide, based on his apparent depressions throughout his life and his failed attempts at finding a wife. But, some historians have debated the possibility of foul play, especially in the late-20th century.

William Clark was born in 1770 in Caroline County, Virginia. In 1784 the Clark family moved to Kentucky to a large tract of land near Louisville. At the age of 19, Clark joined the Kentucky Militia, then transferred to the regular U.S. Army as an ensign and advanced to the rank of lieutenant. He resigned from the army in 1796 to attend to family business. At the time of the Expedition's departure Clark was 34 years old.

Although seen as equal and inseparable in the eyes of most Americans, Lewis and Clark were quite different in temperament. Although intellectually gifted, Lewis had trouble with day-to-day tasks and responsibilities. He was quiet and moody, did not enjoy the company of many people, and could be impatient, demanding and aloof. By sharing his command with William Clark, Lewis found a perfect complement to his own limitations. Clark enjoyed the company of others, and worked well with the enlisted men. He kept the journals even at times that Lewis did not, and also charted the Corps' courses and distances in a remarkable series of highly accurate maps.

After Lewis's death Clark served successfully as governor of the Missouri Territory and Superintendent of Indian Affairs for the West. He married and had a total of seven children. When Clark died in 1838 he was honored with a huge funeral and buried in St. Louis.

WILLIAM CLARK / MICHAEL HAYNES

and whiskey for its survival. Like astronauts on the launching pad, the Corps of Discovery settled in for the winter and waited. They were still linked to the United States and the world as they knew it by the umbilical cords of the U.S. Mail service, army supply lines and medical assistance.

But waiting would be tedious. The work of exploration could not be conducted, yet more than 40 men would have to be kept busy if they were to stay out of trouble. The most important aspect of the winter at Wood River was the task William Clark set for himself: to build from a disparate set of volunteers a cohesive military unit fit for exploration.

With a few exceptions, most of the men at Camp River Dubois had never met each other before joining the Expedition. Lewis and Clark, for instance, knew one another before the trip. There were also two brothers, Joseph and Reubin Field, and two other men, Charles Floyd and Nathaniel Pryor, who were cousins. Some had served in the same army regiments together, but most were strangers to one another. The youngest man, George Shannon, was 17 years old, the oldest, John Shields, was 35. The average age of the men was 27.

Lewis, meanwhile, spent most of the winter either in Cahokia or St. Louis. This was typical of military billeting during of the period. Lewis, as the overall commander, took a well-appointed house where he could comfortably hold meetings, conduct correspondence, and avoid the day-to-day problems presented by the men. Lewis also bought supplies in St. Louis, including corn, flour, barrels of salt, kegs of pork, boxes of candles, hog's oil (lard), and 21 bales of Indian goods and tools. Not only did he procure supplies, he ingratiated himself with the locals. Most of the $15,011 that Lewis spent went to local merchants, who hired

MISSOURI HISTORICAL SOCIETY, ST. LOUIS / PHOTO BY BOB LITTLE, ALLIED PHOTOCOLOR

William Clark's pocket compass, set in glass in a field of jasper, was attached to a gold chain.

Celebrating the 29th Independence Day

It was Wednesday, July 4, 1804, near present-day Atchison County, Kansas. The day started with a blast from the bowpiece, the swivel gun, of the keelboat. For only the second time at this point in the Expedition, the men named a site that they had passed. They called it Independence Day Creek or Fourth of July Creek. The day had ended the same way as it started – another discharge of the bowpiece. That night, the men got an extra gill of whiskey and they danced to celebrate. The United States was 28 years old.

This is not written in the journals, but this is the way it probably happened. The men might have actually stood in formation, and performed a bit of close-order drill. And, there might have been an inspection in ranks. Very likely they fired off a volley as a salute to their country's birthday. It is likely the commanders gave a short speech on the first Fourth of July celebration west of the Mississippi.

The French boatmen, on the other hand, probably stood off on the side and wondered just a little bit about this upstart country, one that was only a generation old. Some of the soldiers celebrating their country's independence were born before their country existed. They were born Englishmen – colonists – subjects of the king. Certainly most were born by the time their country had earned its independence.

This was an expansive country, until March 10 stretching from the Atlantic Coast to the Mississippi River, but populated by just 5.3 million people. And two-thirds of that population lived within 50 miles of the tidewater. With just four poor roads crossing the Appalachian Mountains, many Americans in the West felt disenfranchised and isolated. Now, that young country was about to extend its reach to the far side of the continent.

– Hal Stearns

Hal Stearns of Wayne, Nebraska, is a lecturer on the Great Plains, American West and Lewis and Clark. He has degrees from Notre Dame University and The University of Montana.

engagés (French boatmen). These men and some additional soldiers would help the permanent party pull the boats up the Missouri in 1804 and then return to St. Louis with reports and discoveries in 1805.

Much of the winter of 1803-04 was focused on the men and their transformation into the Corps of Discovery. Clark kept the men busy at all times. First, they cut a road a mile long through the timber, then built a fort and cabins out of logs. Clark drilled them, teaching them how to march in formation, use their weapons as a team and shoot effectively at targets. Clark and Sergeant John Ordway tried to get the men to respect military authority and learn to follow orders. When they would later face danger on the frontier, there would be no time for the men to question their officers. In effect, Clark ran a boot camp that weeded out misfits and troublemakers and put great pressure on the various members of the Corps to conform to military rules and regulations.

Each man was expected to shave at least once every three days and to keep his hair cut short. Pay was low; privates made $5 per month, corporals $6, and sergeants $8. Daily rations consisted of one pound of bread, a pound of beef or pork, a gill of whiskey (one-quarter pint), one-half pint of dried peas or beans, and vinegar to prevent scurvy. Corn meal, beans, sugar, lard, salt, tea and coffee were also available.

Winter Camp Tests Corps Discipline

Each soldier was issued one woolen blanket, and the barracks were heated by open fireplaces, which were also used for cooking and provided most of the light in the room. Reveille was at sunrise and lights were out by 8 or 9 p.m. Only George Drouillard and York, so far as is known, would have been exempt from the regimen at Camp River Dubois, since they were not enlisted in the army. The men in the camp probably longed for a pass to a town like St. Louis, but none were issued. Life in camp was boring and the work and constant drill difficult. The men were probably impatient to get on with the adventure.

As a result, they got drunk and often fought with one another. They were getting extra liquor from enterprising locals who set up a grog shop nearby. Private Whitehouse was in trouble all through the winter and Privates Potts and Werner had a fistfight on January 3. There were thefts of public property and the property of others, and Private Willard Leakins was caught stealing on February 4.

The most common forms of discipline included flogging, a brutal punishment inflicted with a rope divided into nine strands, each tied off at the end with a simple knot. A man could receive up to 100 lashes with this "cat 'o nine tails." Usually, 100 lashes could not be inflicted all in one day, as it might threaten the life of the soldier, so they were administered over two to four successive days.

At Camp River Dubois, however, Clark did not resort to the lash, but instead applied creative punishment. As punishment for fighting, Potts and Werner were ordered to build a hut together for the laundress, forcing men who had been fighting to cooperate with one another. Theft simply was not tolerated. On February 4, 1804, the same day he was caught stealing, Private Leakins was discharged from the Expedition.

In late-February, feeling that the men were on a good footing, Clark left the camp in charge of Sergeant Ordway. When he returned a week later he cited Reubin Field, John Colter, John Boley, Peter Weiser and John Robertson for infractions ranging from defying the sergeant's orders to stand guard duty to leaving the post in search of whiskey.

Instead of handing out strong punishment, however, Clark merely confined the culprits to camp for ten days, which differed little from the norm of their lives. Why such leniency for such serious offenses? Perhaps Clark saw a silver lining. The four men who went AWOL from the camp did not know one another before living at Wood River. They were now working together – even if in mischief.

On March 9, 1804, Lewis attended a ceremony in St. Louis, during which the

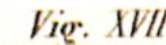

BEAVER HUT ON THE MISSOURI/KARL BODMER

Upper Louisiana Territory was transferred from Spain to France to the United States. Now all the land from the Mississippi River to the tops of the Rocky Mountains was officially, at least in the eyes of Europeans and Euroamericans, U.S. soil. Lewis must have been proud to see the flag of his country raised over St. Louis, and eager to get on with the trip for which he had made such careful preparations.

On March 31, 1804, Lewis and Clark selected the men for the Expedition and chose its sergeants. Ordway remained a sergeant, and Pryor and Floyd were promoted to that rank. Between 35 and 40 men were living at Camp River Dubois on March 31; 25 of these men were chosen for the permanent party.

On May 6, Clark received some disheartening news. His commission as a captain, promised by Lewis and Jefferson, had not come through. Instead, Clark was appointed a second lieutenant. This was an insult to a man who had previously

Prized furbearers, beavers were often noted in the Lewis and Clark journals. On his 34th birthday on August 1, 1804, Clark wrote, "This being my birth day I order'd a Saddle of fat Vennison, an Elk fleece & Bevertail to be cooked and a Desert of Cheries, Plumbs, Raspberries Currents and grapes of a Supr. quallity."

Meriwether Lewis's silver watch with a second hand was made by Peter Desvignes in London in the late-1790s. It is now part of the Missouri Historical Society Museum collection in St. Louis.

MISSOURI HISTORICAL SOCIETY, ST. LOUIS / GLENN S. HENSLEY PHOTO

held the rank of first lieutenant, and Lewis was mortified because he had given his word that Clark would share rank with him. Lewis never told the men there was any difference in rank between himself and Clark; the two men were considered by the soldiers to be co-captains, with equal powers and authority, for the entire journey.

On May 14, 1804, the Expedition began at Wood River, with Clark in command. Lewis joined the Corps of Discovery in St. Charles, Missouri a week later. The outbound party numbered at least 46, and included 34 young, unmarried soldiers, the civilian interpreter and hunter, George Drouillard, Clark's slave, York, and even Lewis's Newfoundland dog, Seaman. The party also included hired French boatmen who would travel only to the Mandan country for the first winter, then return to St. Louis.

The country they passed through the first few weeks of the voyage had been traversed for nearly 100 years by French and Spanish explorers and traders. The Corps had reliable maps of this section of the river, and was on the lookout for well-known landmarks.

Moving Upriver: An Exhausting and Difficult Task

Travel up the Missouri River in 1804 was difficult and exhausting work because heat, injuries and insects. The river was troublesome, too, with its strong current and floating logs and trees. These obstacles, or snags, driven by the current, could sink a boat.

The boats were propelled in a variety of ways, including sails, oars and long poles. Sometimes the boats had to be pulled upriver with ropes by men walking along the shoreline, a procedure called "cordelling." The party averaged 10 to 15 miles per day.

When they stopped for the evening, two musicians in the group, Pierre Cruzatte and George Gibson, brought out their fiddles. Some of the men had enough energy to dance and sing along by the light of the campfires.

Usually two men designated as hunters foraged inland, flushing out game for the stew pot and transporting it back to the river on the backs of two horses. George Drouillard was the permanent hunter, augmented by a rotation of promising recruits, who he tutored in the ways of the woods one at a time. Theirs was an essential task, because each man on the trek, sweating and straining to move the boats against the current, consumed nine to ten pounds of meat a day.

As they moved up the Missouri, several members of the Expedition recorded events in their journals. Lewis, unfortunately, does not seem to have been one of them. For some reason, perhaps because the terrain they were seeing was so well known, Lewis kept only sporadic scientific notes. Our knowledge of this portion of the voyage comes from the journals of William Clark, John Ordway, Joseph Whitehouse, Patrick Gass and Charles Floyd. Although Robert Frazer kept a journal, it has been lost. The surviving journals provide a somewhat terse and undetailed account of the first two months of the Expedition.

On May 23, Whitehouse noted that the Expedition passed "Boons settlement lying on the North side of the River. This settlement was made by Colonel Daniel Boone, the person who first discover'd Kentucky, & who was residing at this place, with a number of his family and friends." Clark noted that Lewis ascended a hill on the south side of the river "and nearly fell from a cliff 300 feet high." He "Saved himself by the assistance of his Knife." This short entry chronicled an event that might have ended the Expedition before it had truly begun.

On May 23, 1804, Meriwether Lewis (right) ascended a cliff 300 feet above the river at Tavern Cave and nearly fell from a peninsula of rocks. Clark wrote, "Saved himself by the assistance of his Knife . . . he caught at 20 feet." Had the knife not held the Expedition might have been ended only a few days after it had begun.

The following day the boats were maneuvered past a dangerous place in the river called, for good reason, the Devil's Race Grounds. "we wer verry near loseing our Boat in Toeing," wrote Clark, for "She Struck the Sands (which is continerly roaling <& turned>) . . . all hand Jumped out on the upper Side and bore on that Side untill the Sand washed from under the boat and wheeled on the next bank. . . the Violence of the Current was so great that the Toe roap Broke, the Boat turned Broadside, as the Current Washed the Sand from under her She

LEWIS ESCAPES DEATH / MICHAEL HAYNES

NODAWAY ISLAND / KARL BODMER

The Corps camped on Nodaway Island on July 8, 1804. Clark estimated the island to be 7,000 or 8,000 acres. The island, located northwest of St. Joseph, Missouri, still exists.

wheeled & lodged on the bank below as often as three times, before we got her in Deep water." Despite this dramatic incident, Ordway wrote only this of the day's events: "nothing remarkable as recollected." On May 25, they passed a small French village of seven families called La Charette. Floyd noted that "This is the Last Setelment of whites on this River."

Lewis was often away from the boats, which were left in the charge of Clark.

As Clark noted on May 31, "Capt Lewis went out to the woods & found many curious Plants & Srubs." Lewis continued the scientific work of the Expedition, identifying animals and plants like the plains horned toad, eastern wood rat, and *Psoralea esculenta,* (prairie apple). Clark occasionally ventured ashore for his turn to survey the countryside. He investigated Indian mounds, paintings on the limestone bluffs, and marveled at the beautiful wooded highlands above the Missouri River floodplain, noting that the land they had passed through was the best he had ever seen, with good timber of oak, ash, hickory, and black walnut.

Almost daily the Expedition was met by fur trappers in canoes, some white, many Indian, and at least one African-American, on their way down the river to

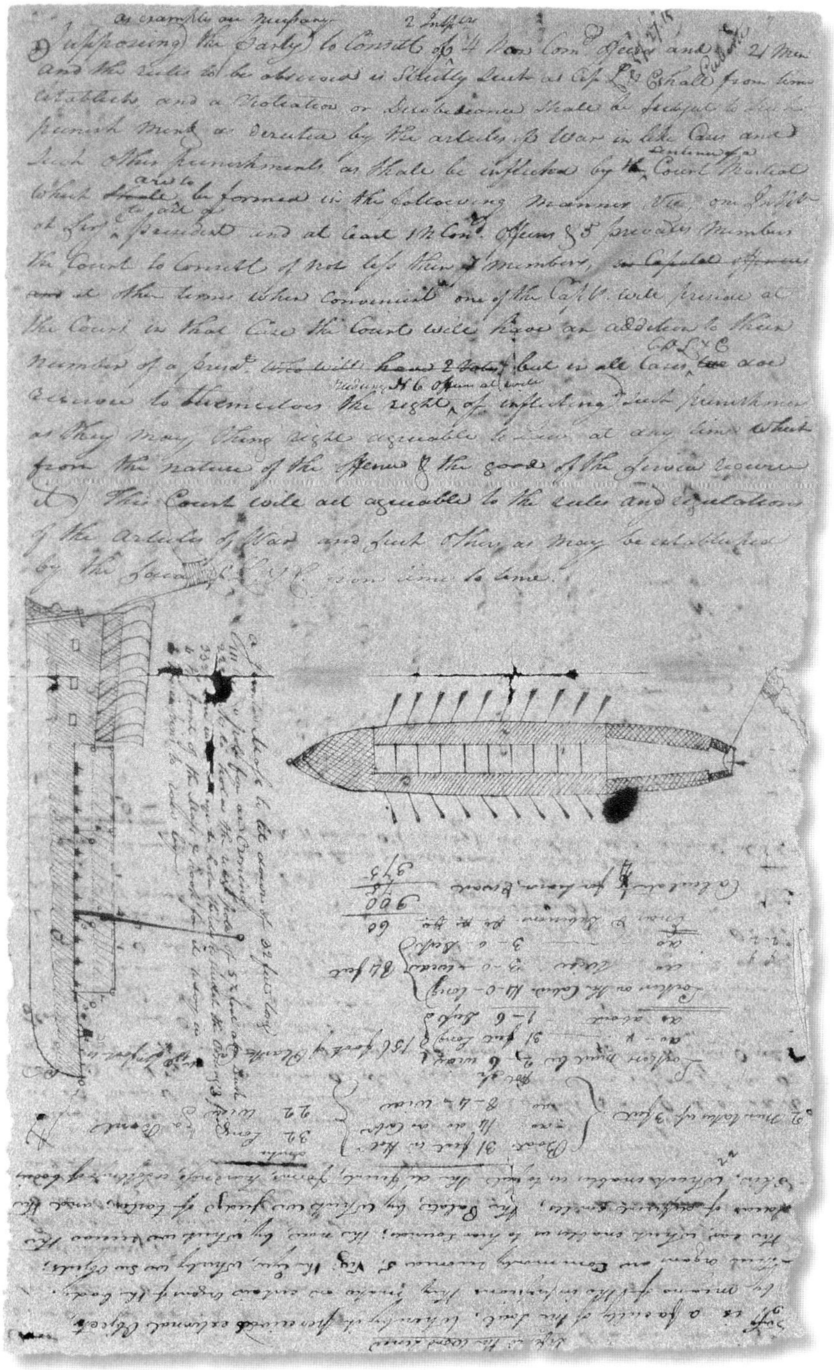

In his journal entry on January 21, 1804, Clark included two sketches of the Expedition's keelboat. The boat was 55-feet long, with an 8-foot beam, and a shallow draft.

trade their winter catch in St. Louis. On June 12, the Corps stopped to chat with traders who had been living with the Yankton Sioux tribe in modern-day South Dakota. Among them was Pierre Dorion, "an old man who had been with the Soux 20 years & had great influence with them," recorded Clark. The captains used their powers of persuasion, convincing Dorion, who was within a couple of days of reaching St. Louis, to return upriver with them to act as a translator and to convince tribal leaders to make an official visit to Washington to meet the president.

The days were filled with drudgery for the men, and the nights probably brought a fitful rest for their sore bodies. On June 17, Clark noted that "The Ticks are numerous and large and have been [troublesome] all the way and the Musquetors are beginning to be verry troublesome . . . the French higherlins Complain for the want of Provisions, Saying they are accustomed to eat 5 & 6 times a day, they are roughly rebuked for their presumption ... The party is much aflicted with Boils and Several have the Decissentary, which I contribute to the water." Whitehouse, walking along the shore with the cordelling line, wrote on June 22 that "The weather proved excessive hot . . . The current running very strong against us, and having to tow the boat, it can hardly be imagined the fatigue that we underwent . . . We Towed [the boat] 12 Miles this day."

From June 26 to 28, the explorers made camp above the mouth of the Kansas River in the area of modern Kansas City, Kansas. They built a temporary fortification of brush and logs across the point formed by the confluence of the Kansas and Missouri rivers, according to Whitehouse "to defend ourselves against the Indians, fearing that they might make an attack on us in the Night." Clark noted that they "Cleaned out the Boat, Suned our Powder, wolen articles [and] examined every thing. 8 or 10 huntrs. out to day in different direction, in examining our private Store of Provisions we found Several articles Spoiled from the wet or dampness they had received. . . our hunters Killed Several Deer and Saw Buffalow." The men were employed in "Dressing Skins & makeing themselves Comfortable." But stopping to rest also invited some of the men to get into trouble. A courts-martial was held on June 29 to try John Collins and Hugh Hall, who stole whiskey from the whiskey barrel while Collins had been assigned to guard it. Collins was given 100 lashes, Hall 50.

Clark: "We Camped in the plain"

The Corps followed the Missouri as it turned north, reaching the site of modern Atchison, Kansas, by July 4. Clark recorded that they "ussered in the day by a discharge of one shot from our Bow piece." They passed a stream that they dubbed Independence Creek, and gave the men an extra gill of whiskey at the end of the day. "We Camped in the plain," noted Clark, "one of the most butifull Plains, I ever Saw, open & butifully diversified with hills & vallies all presenting themselves to the river covered with grass and a few scattering trees, a handsom Creek meandering thro. . . Groops of Shrubs covered with the most delicious froot is to be seen in every direction, and nature appears to have exerted herself to butify the Senery by the variety of flours . . . raised above the Grass, which Strikes & profumes the sensations, and amuses the mind." Whitehouse, meanwhile, on the other end of the social scale from the captains, nursed his tired body and sore feet, probably grateful for the extra liquor to numb his pain. "the day mighty hot. . . we left off rowing and went to Towing the boat, but the sand was so hot, that it scalded our feet, some of the Men left the tow rope, and had to put on their Mockasins to keep their feet from being burnt. . . "

On July 10, they made camp in Holt County, Missouri, across from the Kansas-Nebraska border. This site was near today's Squaw Creek National Wildlife Refuge, which exhibits some of the terrain and wildlife noted by the men of the Expedition. Ordway noted the change in terrain: "on the South Side is a beuautiful Bottom prarie which will contain about 2000 acres of Land covered with wild rye and wild potatoes. . . the Bottoms on the north Side is very extensive & thick the hills

INDEPENDENCE DAY ON THE MISSOURI RIVER / RICK REEVES

or high Land is near the River on [the] South Side & are but thinly timbered. back of those hills is open prarie." The Corps had reached the tallgrass prairies of the Great Plains. From here on the land would take on a character different from what most of them had ever seen before. Meanwhile, they were becoming a team, overcoming the daily difficulties of travel and moving each day in measured but deliberate increments toward their goal. Their voyage was just beginning, but they would be ready for the dangers, hardships and triumphs that lay ahead.

To celebrate July 4th in 1804, Captains Lewis and Clark donned their dress uniforms and ordered a salute fired by the gun on the keelboat. This scene took place opposite Independence Creek about 25 miles north of the future site of Fort Leavenworth.

Key Members of the Expedition

By Bob Moore

KEN BOUC

Much of the attention on the Corps of Discovery has been focused on its captains, Meriwether Lewis and William Clark. But, other members played key roles, too.

Some were recruited especially for the journey, while others volunteered for the Expedition from the U.S. Army or were hired because of their specific talents. Their median age was about 27, and they hailed equally from the northern, southern and western parts of the infant United States. These are profiles of some principal members of the Corps.

Charles Floyd

The Corps of Discovery was compiled in a makeshift fashion from several different pools of men. One group of volunteers from Kentucky, Indiana and Pennsylvania, recruited by Lewis and Clark in the summer of 1803, has become known as the "nine young men from Kentucky." It included Charles Floyd, who was born in Kentucky about 1782, and was only 22 years old when recruited for the Expedition. He was a cousin of Nathaniel Pryor, and may have been distantly related to Clark.

The captains were impressed with Floyd's abilities and appointed him as one of the three original sergeants. Floyd is best known as the Expedition's only fatality, dying on August 20, 1804, probably of a burst appendix. It's not clear whether Floyd died on the Nebraska or Iowa side of the river, but he was buried on a bluff near today's Sioux City, Iowa. A 100-foot obelisk today marks the site.

Nathaniel Hale Pryor

Another of the original sergeants was Nathaniel Hale Pryor, who was born in Virginia in 1772 and moved to Kentucky in 1783. He might have kept a journal on the Expedition, but none has ever been found.

At the conclusion of the Expedition the captains helped Pryor get a commission as an officer in the U.S. Army. In 1807 he led an expedition up the Missouri River to return Mandan chief Big White to his people. The Arikaras attacked Pryor's party and wounded or killed several men. Pryor rose to the rank of captain in the army and served in the Battle of New Orleans in 1815.

After the war Pryor settled along the Arkansas River, becoming a trader to the Osage. He died on June 1, 1831, and is buried in Pryor, Oklahoma, where a monument stands in his honor.

John Ordway

John Ordway was the only sergeant recruited directly from the U.S. Army. He was born about 1775 in Dumbarton, New Hampshire. By 1803 he was serving as a sergeant in the 1st Infantry Regiment at Fort Kaskaskia, Illinois, where he met Lewis and Clark. The captains relied upon Ordway's military experience to maintain the efficiency of the Corps during their winter encampment of 1803-1804.

Ordway traveled all the way to the Pacific Ocean and returned, making an entry in his journal every day of the trip. Although it was lost for more than 100 years, his journal was discovered in 1916 and published.

Ordway returned to Missouri to settle in 1809, became prosperous and married. The Ordways had no children, and both he and his wife had died by 1817.

Patrick Gass

Patrick Gass was born in Falling Springs, Pennsylvania, on June 12, 1771, and learned the carpenter's trade from his father. He was serving with the 1st Infantry Regiment at Fort Kaskaskia when Lewis and Clark arrived in 1803. Gass was then 32 years old.

He stood about five-feet, seven-inches tall, had a barrel-chest, dark complexion, gray eyes and dark hair. After Sergeant Floyd died, Gass was elected to take his place. His journal of the Expedition was the first to be published, in 1807. Gass stayed in the army and served in the War of 1812. He was discharged after he lost his left eye in an accident at Fort Independence in 1815, and settled in Wellsburg, West Virginia. When Gass was 60 years old he married 20-year-old Maria Hamilton. They had six children. He died April 2, 1870, at age 98, the last known survivor of the Expedition.

George Drouillard

Usually written "Drewyer" in the journals, George Drouillard was born in Michigan Territory or Canada about 1773. His father was French and his mother was Shawnee, and he went to live with his mother's people in the Cape Girardeau District of Missouri while still a boy. Drouillard was skilled at several Indian dialects and sign language, and was very handy with a rifle.

He joined the Expedition at Fort Massac, Illinois, as an interpreter, and was paid $25 per month. Drouillard was trusted with all the most difficult assignments of the Expedition, including the pursuit of deserters La Liberté and Moses Reed in 1804 and the exploration of the Marias River with Lewis in 1806.

After the return of the Expedition, Drouillard became a partner in Manuel Lisa's fur trading ventures on the upper Missouri. Drouillard and two Shawnee companions were killed near the post by a party of Blackfeet in 1810.

Joseph and Reubin Field

The brothers Joseph and Reubin Field became, along with George Drouillard, Lewis's most dependable men. Reubin Field was born in Virginia in 1771, and Joseph a year later. Their family moved to Kentucky when they were very young. Both were excellent hunters and crack shots. Reubin was known as the Expedition's fastest runner.

They accompanied Drouillard and Lewis on the reconnaissance of the Marias River in 1806, where they had a fight with a Blackfeet war party that tried to take their rifles and horses. Reubin stabbed one of the Indians to death. Joseph died less than a year after the Expedition returned. Reubin settled in Little Bee Lick, Kentucky, married in 1808, and died by early-1823. Neither brother had children.

John Colter

John Colter is probably the only member of the Expedition whose fame does not rest solely on service with the Corps of Discovery. He was born near Staunton in Augusta County, Virginia, about 1775 and later moved to Maysville, Kentucky. He stood five-feet, ten-inches tall, had blue eyes and was rather shy.

Colter was a discipline problem at Camp Wood, but later turned out to be a reliable member of the Expedition and an excellent hunter. On the return journey Colter received permission to leave the party and join a small trapping expedition headed back up the Missouri. He later became the first non-Indian to see what is now Yellowstone National Park. After a couple of close calls with the Blackfeet, Colter returned to Missouri, settled on a farm near Bridgeton, married and had two children. Colter died of an illness during service in the War of 1812.

Pierre Cruzatte, Francois Labiche, Jean Baptiste Lepage

There were also at least three half-French, half-Indian soldiers recruited for the Corps. They included Pierre Cruzatte, an experienced boatman who was blind in one eye and nearsighted in the other. Cruzatte often entertained the men of the Expedition with his fiddle. On the return voyage in 1806, Cruzatte mistakenly shot Lewis in the behind. Cruzatte later worked in the fur trade and was killed by Indians before 1828.

Francois Labiche was a good boatman, Indian trader and interpreter. He later lived in or near St. Louis and raised seven children.

Jean Baptiste Lepage joined the Expedition at the Mandan Villages in 1805, and traveled to the Pacific Ocean with Lewis and Clark. Like many of the members of the Corps of Discovery, little else is known about him.

John Shields

John Shields was born in Harrisonburg, Augusta County, Virginia, in 1769. His family emigrated to Pigeon Forge in Tennessee in 1784, where he established a mill and a blacksmith shop. Shields had a wife, Nancy, and a daughter, Janette, before he joined the Expedition.

At 35, he was probably the oldest member of the Corps of Discovery. His skills at blacksmithing, gunsmithing and carpentry were invaluable to the party, and after the Expedition Lewis asked that Congress pay him a bonus for his services to the Corps. Shields trapped in Missouri for a time with Daniel Boone, who was a relative, then settled in Indiana, where he died in December 1809.

George Shannon

One of the most successful of the "nine young men" after the Expedition ended was George Shannon. Born in 1785 in Claysville, Pennsylvania, Shannon was the youngest member of the party at 17.

In the autumn of 1804, he was lost for over two weeks and almost starved to death. In 1807, Shannon went along with Nathaniel Pryor's expedition to return Chief Big White to the Mandans and lost a leg in a fight with the Arikara. Shannon was a major contributor to Nicholas Biddle's 1814 edition of the journals.

He married in 1813, studied law in Lexington, Kentucky, and moved to St. Charles, Missouri, where he had his practice. He served as U.S. Attorney for the District of Missouri and also in the Missouri State Senate. Shannon died in Palmyra, Missouri, in 1836 at age 51.

The Plains Commence

By Jay H. Buckley

The Expedition left the more wooded, well-known lower Missouri, and entered a strange new land of endless grass. Here, they found new species, held councils with Indians, punished lapses in discipline and buried a comrade.

THE CORPS OF DISCOVERY awakened to a damp morning on July 14, 1804. Rain had fallen all night and the wetness delayed departure until 7 a.m. A half-hour later, an ominous black cloud blew in, accompanied by wind and rain that pummeled the 55-foot keelboat and two pirogues. Unable to seek safety on either shore – because of banks caving in on one side and snags lining the other – the men anchored the keelboat midstream and braced for the squall to pass.

White-capped waves broke over the gunwales as wind tossed the craft, nearly pushing it onto a sandbar island. The men jumped overboard on the leeward side and put their shoulders to the hull to keep the keelboat from running aground. After 40 minutes, an eerie calm suddenly fell over the river and it became as smooth as glass.

The Corps had been traveling the Missouri River a little more than a week since it had shifted from a westerly course to a more northerly one. Although exhausted by the stifling summer heat and their struggle against the muddy current, the men noticed a change in the beautiful landscape. Away from the river, the hills flattened out and the trees thinned, often giving way to lush prairie grasses. On Tuesday, July 10, just below the present Nebraska-Kansas border and the mouth of the Big Nemaha River, Clark wrote in his journal that, just beyond the hills, "the Plains Commence."

From the mouth of the Big Nemaha River, where they camped the next two days, until their arrival at the Niobrara River's confluence with the Missouri on September 4, the Lewis and Clark Expedition ascended the Missouri with present-day Nebraska on its left, and what would become Missouri, Iowa and South Dakota on its right.

During these two months the party entered an environment filled with new species of flora and fauna, witnessed the death of a comrade, dealt with the mission's most serious disciplinary issue, and held its first council with native people.

Jay H. Buckley is an assistant professor of history and director of the Native American Studies Program at Brigham Young University in Provo, Utah. He is writing a biography of William Clark. Buckley earned a doctorate in history at the University of Nebraska-Lincoln, where Gary Moulton was his advisor. While at UNL, Buckley worked at the Center for Great Plains Studies.

MOUTH OF THE PLATTE RIVER 900 MILES ABOVE ST. LOUIS / GEORGE CATLIN

Scientific Discoveries

As the Expedition headed northward on July 4, Clark saw that "The Plains of this countrey are covered with a Leek Green Grass [big bluestem *(Andropogon gerardi)*], well calculated for the sweetest and most norushing hay." Within a month, this towering western grass would reach heights of eight to 12 feet. Clumps of trees, pools of water and shrubbery covered with delicious fruit stretched before them, as if Mother Nature was determined to beautify the landscape with sweet-smelling flowers and "So magnificent a Senerey."

On July 12 from the top of an Indian mound near the mouth of the Big Nemaha River, Clark "had an extensive view of the Serounding Plains, which afforded one of the most pleasing prospects I ever beheld." Walking on the Nebraska shore

In a painting made in 1832, artist George Catlin assumed an aerial vantage point, above a group of Indians on a bluff, to show a panoramic view of the confluence of the Platte and Missouri rivers.

BLACKBIRD'S GRAVE ON THE MISSOURI RIVER 1100 MILES ABOVE ST. LOUIS / GEORGE CATLIN

near present-day Omaha, Clark recorded that about a mile distant from the river the country was "one Continued Plain as fur as Can be seen."

The beautiful landscape of the Great Plains received frequent mention in Expedition journals. Bald loess hills with occasional timber near the river extended from the east bank. To the west, a beautiful rolling prairie of waving grass stretched before them. On July 20 on Nebraska's Weeping Water Creek, they chronicled that "The Soil of Those Praries appears rich but much Parched with the frequent fires." In addition to fires started by lightning, Indians set fire to the Plains to signal others. Fire renewed the prairie and suppressed the trees, which attracted game and provided forage for Indian ponies.

A river ran through it, and President Jefferson understood the importance and value of rivers. He envisioned the Missouri as the most practical and direct water route across the continent, a vital commercial avenue for the expanding American fur trade. Longer than the Mississippi and draining an immense watershed, the Missouri flowed out of the Rocky Mountains. Jefferson hoped its headwaters would be but a short portage to the source of the Columbia River, although this would later prove wishful thinking. For the time being, however, finding the fabled Northwest Passage seemed a distant problem, while simply ascending the Missouri was the more immediate challenge.

When the Expedition reached the mouth of the Platte River on July 21, it left the lower Missouri and entered its middle reaches. Clark wrote that "This Great river [the Platte] being much more rapid than the Missourie forces its [the Missouri's] current against the opposit Shore, . . . we found great dificuelty in passing around the Sand at the mouth of this River." Lewis, Clark and six men

On August 11, 1804, Lewis and Clark and a party of 10 men climbed 300 feet above the Missouri River, near the present-day line between Thurston and Burt counties in Nebraska, to Blackbird Hill. They planted a flag on the grave site of Omaha Indian Chief Blackbird, who had died in about 1800 of smallpox along with hundreds of others in his tribe. Returning from the hill, Clark noted, " . . . the river may be Seen Meandering for 60 or 70 Miles."

One of the bends he saw is now cut off from the river and forms Badger Lake State Wildlife Management Area in Iowa. The next day at noon Clark sent a man overland to the previous day's lunch site. He measured the isthmus at 974 yards, but the Corps had taken the 18¾-mile river course – a day's travel. (A modern aerial photograph of the Badger Lake oxbow is on page 120.)

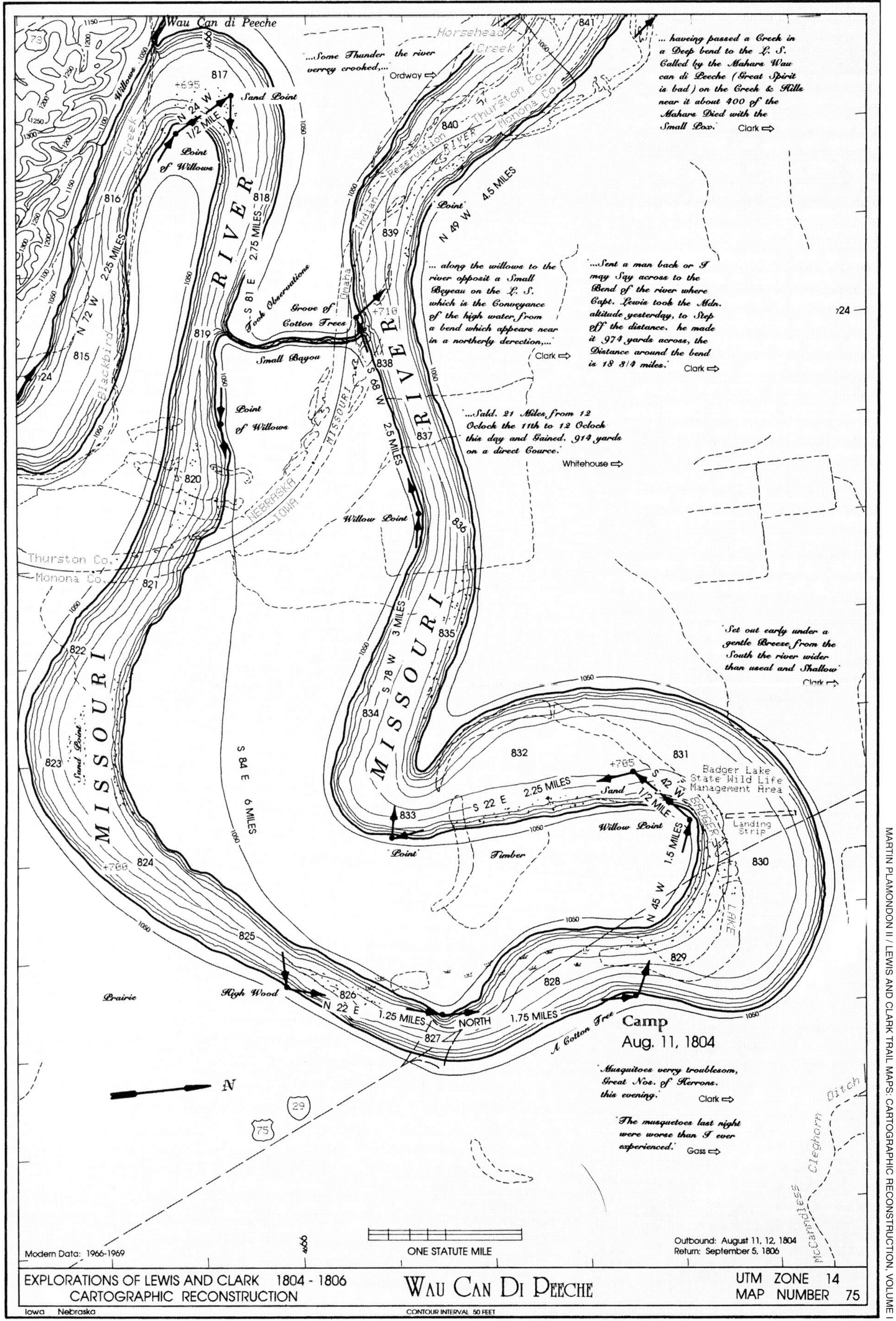
Wau Can di Peeche
"...Some Thunder the river verrey crooked,..." Ordway
"... haveing passed a Creek in a Deep bend to the L. S. Called by the Mahars Wau can di Peeche (Great Spirit is bad) on the Creek & Hills near it about 400 of the Mahars Died with the Small Pox." Clark
"... along the willows to the river opposit a Small Bayeau on the L. S. which is the Conveyance of the high water from a bend which appears near in a northerly derection,..." Clark
"...Sent a man back or I may Say across to the Bend of the river where Capt. Lewis took the Mdn. altitude yesterday, to Step off the distance. he made it 974 yards across, the Distance around the bend is 18 3/4 miles." Clark
"...Sald. 21 Miles from 12 Oclock the 11th to 12 Oclock this day and Gained, 914 yards on a direct Cource." Whitehouse
"Set out early under a gentle Breeze from the South the river wider than useal and Shallow" Clark
"Musquitoes verry troublesom, Great Nos. of Herrons. this evening." Clark
"The musquetoes last night were worse than I ever experienced." Gass
Camp
Aug. 11, 1804
Sand Point
Point of Willows
Grove of Cotton Trees
Took Observations
Small Bayou
Willow Point
High Wood
Prairie
Timber
A Cotton Tree
MISSOURI
RIVER
Horsehead Creek
Blackbird Creek
Willow Creek
Thurston Co.
Monona Co.
NEBRASKA
IOWA
Omaha Indian Reservation
Badger Lake State Wild Life Management Area
Landing Strip
Cleghorn Ditch
McCandless
N 24 W 1/2 MILE
N 72 W 2.25 MILES
S 81 E 2.75 MILES
S 89 W 2.5 MILES
N 49 W 4.5 MILES
S 78 W 3 MILES
S 84 E 6 MILES
S 22 E 2.25 MILES
S 42 W 1/2 MILE
N 45 W 1.5 MILES
N 22 E 1.25 MILES
NORTH 1.75 MILES
N
ONE STATUTE MILE
Modern Data: 1966-1969
Outbound: August 11, 12, 1804
Return: September 5, 1806
EXPLORATIONS OF LEWIS AND CLARK 1804 - 1806
CARTOGRAPHIC RECONSTRUCTION
WAU CAN DI PEECHE
UTM ZONE 14
MAP NUMBER 75
Iowa Nebraska
CONTOUR INTERVAL 50 FEET

One of the most fascinating yet enigmatic figures of the Lewis and Clark Expedition was William Clark's slave York. He was the only member who had no choice about whether or not he would go. As a slave, he was bound to do what he was told by his master, yet as a member of the Corps of Discovery, he participated fully in one of the seminal events of American history. York and Clark probably grew up together, and were about the same age. York was a large man, perhaps a little overweight, and very strong.

Trouble began between Clark and York after the Expedition. York apparently asked Clark for his freedom, citing his good services during the Expedition and his wish to live with his wife in Kentucky. Clark refused until after 1816. Clark later reported that York died of cholera in Tennessee before 1832.

YORK / MICHAEL HAYNES

ascended the Platte in a pirogue for several miles before turning back.

Significant stands of timber had become scarcer since the mouth of the Big Nemaha, so much so that they rated mention in the journals when encountered. As the boats passed the Platte, Clark began looking for a place to rest the men for a few days, a place "Calculated to make our party Comfortable in a Situation where they Could receive the benefit of Shade." They did not find the timber they sought in the campsite that night, July 21, near the mouth of Papillion Creek in Sarpy County, Nebraska. They found their shade the next day at a place Clark would name "White Catfish Camp."

Clark masterfully chronicled the Missouri River's course and served as the Expedition's principal cartographer. He proved an exceptionally gifted maker of maps and created nearly 200. His notation of key geographical features, detailed charts of the course of the Missouri and its tributaries, and his judgment of distance proved exceptionally accurate.

On July 23, while waiting at White Catfish Camp for a possible Indian delegation to arrive, Clark started "Coppying a Map of the river below to Send

NEWFOUNDLAND DOG / PHILIP REINAGLE

This 1802 depiction of a Newfoundland shows a different dog than today's breed standard.

"Our Dog" Seaman

A Newfoundland dog named Seaman accompanied the Corps of Discovery. Captain Meriwether Lewis purchased his "very active, strong, and docile" companion for $20 in the eastern United States. As the Corps traveled up the Missouri River, Seaman's contributions made him a valued member of the group. Soon all referred to him as "our dog."

Newfoundland dogs of the early-19th century were black and white, gangly, hard-working, water dogs descended from retrievers and shepherds brought to eastern Canada by French and English colonists. Clearly possessing a combination of traits from his forebears, Seaman was a strong swimmer, exceptional hunter and stalwart guard.

Floating down the Ohio River to meet William Clark, Lewis wrote that: "I made my dog take as many [squirrels] each day as I had occasion for, they swim very light on the water and make pretty good speed my dog would take the squirrel[s] in the water kill them and swimming bring them in his mouth to the boat." Seaman later hunted pronghorns and deer the same way, by overtaking them "attempting to swim the river," drowning them and dragging them back to shore.

Occasionally, Seaman hunted beaver. In one incident, he almost died when a "beaver bit him through the hind leg and cut the artery; it was with great difficulty that [Lewis] could stop the blood." Journal entries show the explorers fretted while their comrade struggled to recover.

Although barely healed, 10 nights later Seaman's instincts were tested when a bull bison stormed into camp. Lewis describes how the enormous beast ran "in full speed directly towards the fires within 18 inches of the heads of some of the men who lay sleeping." Seaman saved them "by causing [the bull] to change his course . . ."

Despite being well cared for, on occasion Seaman disappeared, only to reappear farther upriver. Once the men were worried when Seaman was gone overnight and "much satisfied" when he returned unhurt the next morning.

While the Corps was headed west on the Columbia River, Seaman impressed a group of Clatsop Indians. Upon the Corps' return the next year, these natives stole Seaman and brought him back to their village. At the prospect of losing his "much prized" associate, Lewis immediately dispatched a small party to retrieve him.

One of the greatest compliments Lewis and company bestowed upon their four-legged companion was noted in the Lewis's July 5, 1806, journal entry. While traveling along the Cokahlahiskit River (today known as the Blackfoot), Lewis described the entrance of a large creek 20 yards wide." He named this tributary Seaman's Creek and the Newfoundland's place in history was assured.

Although not mentioned in the journals after July 15, 1806 at the Great Falls of the Missouri, Seaman probably survived the journey. How, after all, could the Expedition's journalists not have recorded a fatal calamity befalling "our dog"?

– Terry Fingerhut

PLAINS GRAY WOLF / JOHN JAMES AUDUBON

On July 20th, 1804, Clark wrote, "I went out above the mouth of this Creek [Weeping Water Creek in Nebraska] and walked the greater part of the day thro: Plains interspesed with Small Groves of Timber on the branches and Some Scattering trees about the head of the runs, I Killed a Verry large yellow wolf." This was probably a gray wolf *(Canis lupus nubilus),* which followed the buffalo herds, and is now extinct.

to the P. [President] U.S." In addition to his numerous, detailed maps charting the Missouri, he also prepared corrections on a general map (see maps on pages 94-97) that Nicholas King had made in 1803 that Clark modified through observation and calculation. This, too, he would send back to the President in the spring of 1805.

Scenery was not all that held the captains' interests. Lewis's training in Philadelphia had prepared him to identify, collect and catalog known and unknown species of animals and plants to send back to Jefferson and scholars in the East.

The tallgrass prairie provided a mosaic of colors as wooded hillsides of oak, walnut, hazelnut, and cottonwood along the river gave way to chokecherries, wild black cherries, plums, grapes, elderberries, gooseberries, and strawberries. Violets, goldenrods, and other blooming flowers burst in an explosion of color. From the Kansas River to the Niobrara, Lewis used his botanical training to identify and add 11 new plants to their herbarium, five of them new to science, including buffaloberry *(Shepherdia argentea)*, found at the mouth of the Niobrara River about September 4, 1804.

Satisfying zoological interests, the captains noted geographical range, color variations, abundance, habitats, and distribution of animals along the way and collected specimens to help scientists classify, catalog, and describe them. The men saw their first beavers *(Castor canadensis missouriensis)* on July 5 when Lewis's dog, Seaman, flushed several from their lodge, and saw them more frequently with each passing day. The abundance of beaver would be the impetus for the fur trade, the initial American expansion into the West.

On July 20, while following a small stream most of the day hunting elk, Clark killed "an emence large yellow wolf." It was likely a new discovery, a prairie gray wolf *(Canis lupus nubilus)*, the now-extinct species of huge gray wolf that followed the buffalo herds. The Frenchmen called the stream "the water which cries," today's Weeping Water Creek in Cass County, Nebraska.

On August 23, Joseph Field killed the Expedition's first buffalo *(Bison bison)* near the present location of Vermillion, South Dakota. Although they had seen buffalo and buffalo sign, the animals had eluded them to this point. Farther upstream, buffalo would roam in immense herds too numerous to count.

Field also brought in an animal none of the party had ever seen. It was about the size of a beaver, with hair like a pig, a head like a dog with short ears, and a tail like a groundhog. The Frenchmen called it a "brarow." Today, we call it a badger *(Taxidea taxus)*.

Lewis killed a bull snake *(Pituophis melanoleucus sayi)* that he mistook for a rattler but that upon further examination, revealed it had "No pison teeth therefore think him perfectly innocent." On another occasion near the Little Sioux River, something large and white covering the water in the distance baffled the men. They found it to be a mass of feathers about 60 yards wide that continued for several miles. The men's curiosity was satisfied when they rounded a bend and saw several thousand white pelicans *(Pelecanus erythrorhynchus)* on an island. Private Silas Goodrich, the Expedition's best fisherman, caught several blue catfish *(Ictalurus furcatus)* on July 29. The boiled-down fat of one of them yielded a quart of oil. On August 16, Goodrich and 12 other men caught 709 fish of various species. A week later, two of the men caught nine catfish weighing a total of about 300 pounds.

On July 29, probably on Boyer Chute Wildlife Management Area just north of present Omaha, they saw evidence of "the ravages of a Dreadfull harican which had passed obliquely across the river from the N.W. to S E about twelve months Since." The tremendous force of a tornado had snapped trees four feet in diameter like twigs and left fallen timber strewn about.

Fortunately, the Expedition never encountered a tornado, but it did face stiff winds on many occasions. On August 23 near Vermillion, South Dakota, flying sand blew "like a Cloud of Smoke from the Bars," obstructing their vision.

AMERICAN WHITE PELICAN / JOHN JAMES AUDUBON

In present-day Burt County, Nebraska, the Corps came upon a puzzling sight on August 8, 1804. For a distance of almost three miles, they found a large mass of white feathers floating on the river surface, nearly covering a width of 60 or 70 yards. The mystery was solved when the explorers came upon a sandbar where 5,000 or 6,000 white pelicans *(Pelecanus erythrorhynchus)* were feeding on fish. After Lewis shot one of the birds, the Expedition came to a halt while Lewis examined it. He had water brought from the river and determined the bird's pouch could hold five gallons of water.

In Sickness and in Health

Lewis and Clark passed along the eastern edge of the Great Plains during the sweltering summer months. On July 7, the temperature climbed to 96 degrees. The heat, coupled with the high humidity of the region, drove the heat index over 100 degrees regularly. Whether using poles, oars, or ropes to move the boats upstream, the men expended tremendous energy against the five mph current, making anywhere from five to 20 miles per day, depending on the wind and weather.

"It is wothey of observation to mention that our party has been much healthier on the Voyage than parties of the Same Number is in any other Situation Tumers have been troublesom to them all," Clark noted on July 20. Other ailments plagued the men, who labored all day in dirty, wet clothing. Infections, lesions, and boils were bad enough, but the incessant biting of ticks, deer flies, and unending hordes of mosquitoes was maddening. The party might have enjoyed the gently evening breeze on July 27, but the thick and troublesome mosquitoes "were rageing all night, Some about the sise of house flias [flies]."

The captains, especially Lewis, applied a variety of medical techniques of the period to combat various afflictions. When symptoms of the ague or malarial fevers arose, quinine extracted from Peruvian, dried bark of trees of the genus *Cinchona* that are native to the Andes, was used to ease the symptoms. A combination of bleeding and purging with laxatives was also used. On August 23, Lewis suffered a mild case of poisoning from tasting minerals that contained an unhealthy dose of something.

One advantage of encountering new plants and wildlife was the diverse diet it provided the men. The party was beginning to run out of condiments like butter. The abundant fruits, berries, and edible plants provided the vitamins necessary to

KEN BOUC

Lewis and Clark gave the Jefferson Peace Medal to Indian leaders as a symbol of friendship from their "chief" in Washington. Other gifts the explorers carried included beads, knives, flint strikers, vermillion paint and hatchet heads.

ward off scurvy, a common affliction of many early expeditions. In addition to the deer and elk brought in by George Drouillard, John Colter, and the other hunters, the Expedition occasionally feasted on catfish and waterfowl. To celebrate his 34th birthday on August 1, Clark dined on a meal fit for a king. The main course of fat venison, elk fleece, and beaver tail was followed by a scrumptious dessert of cherries, plums, raspberries, currents, grapes, apples, gooseberries, and hazelnuts.

On this stretch of the journey, Sergeant Charles Floyd became ill and died. He was the first U.S. soldier to be buried west of the Mississippi. In the 2½-year Expedition fraught with dangers of attack, rattlesnakes, grizzlies, and the cold,

WITH ALL THE HONORS OF WAR / MICHAEL HAYNES

Floyd was the party's only casualty on the journey.

In late-July, Floyd had been quite sick, but he recovered enough that his illness did not receive further comment in the journals for several weeks. Then, on August 19, he became deathly ill, and died the following day in the early afternoon. A funeral detail carried his body, wrapped in a blanket, up a hill overlooking the Missouri and buried him with full military honors, A red cedar post was erected to mark the spot. Historians have speculated the 22-year-old Floyd died of either peritonitis (a ruptured appendix) or some sort of intestinal infection, neither of which could have been cured by the doctors or medical

The Expedition's passage up the Missouri River in 1804 was marred by the death of Sergeant Charles Floyd – the only member of the Corps to die on the journey – near present-day Sioux City, Iowa. Floyd probably died as the result of an infected appendix. Clark wrote, "he was buried with the Honors of War much lamented."

MISSOURI INDIAN / OTO INDIAN / CHIEF OF THE PUNCAS / KARL BODMER

Karl Bodmer painted portraits of (from left) a Missouria, an Oto and a Ponca in 1834. The Corps of Discovery met with with Missouria and Oto tribes, but the Poncas were away hunting when the explorers passed by on the Missouri River in 1804.

technology of the period.

The men elected Private Patrick Gass to replace their fallen sergeant and the captains concurred, promoting Gass a few days later to fill the vacancy.

On August 26, near the present site of Newcastle, Nebraska, Private George Shannon failed to return from a hunting trip and a search party could not find him. Shannon, the youngest and least-experienced member of the party, believed the boats had passed him by and quickly headed upstream to catch them. He pursued the elusive boats for 16 days, surviving on berries and a single rabbit he shot using a stick as a projectile because he had run out of rifle balls. Exhausted and weak from hunger, Shannon finally sat down on the riverbank, perhaps hoping to catch a party of trappers or traders hurrying downstream to St. Louis before winter. He gazed out across the shortgrass plains, his bullets wasted, his nerve gone, his luck running out, and wondered whether or not to eat his horse to survive.

Indian Encounters and Councils

With nearly $700 worth of Indian presents loaded in the keelboat, Lewis and Clark hoped to establish friendly relations between the United States and the numerous Indian tribes living in the West. They had brought tokens of empire to distribute to the principal Indian leaders, including flags, uniforms and medals with a likeness of President Jefferson on the front and the motto Peace and Friendship on the reverse side.

The success of the Expedition rested largely on the captains' success in establishing friendly relationships and opening the door for future American trading ventures. Presents of vermillion paint, glass beads, knives, kettles, and fishhooks provided a sampling of American traders' wares. After purchasing goods in St. Louis, the captains divided them before packing them into waterproof bags. Clark doubted that the presents would be enough for the many Indians they would meet, and he was right. They did not bring enough. The Expedition never ran out of powder and lead, or paper and ink, but it ran out of Indian presents about the time it reached the Pacific and needed them most.

Lewis and Clark were not the first Europeans or Americans to pass through the homelands of the Otos, Missourias, Omahas, Iowas, Pawnees, Poncas, and Yanktons. In the 1700s French and Spanish explorers had passed nearby and were later followed by Spanish and French fur traders. In the 1790s, Scotsman James Mackay and his lieutenant John Evans had traveled north from Louisiana as far as the Omaha villages, near Homer in Nebraska today, to established a trading post, Fort Charles. It was abandoned in 1796.

In fact, contact with explorers and traders in the late-1700s brought disaster to the native peoples of the region. Repeated epidemics of smallpox, the most recent in 1800, had swept along the Missouri, greatly reducing populations living near the river and it was a primary reason the Corps had difficulty making contact with the tribes. The Corps saw the abandoned villages and burial mounds, and would later visit Ton won tonga, the once large Omaha village near present Homer, Nebraska, where some 400 men, women, and children had perished a few years before.

It must have been a time of great anticipation for the two captains, eager to fine-tune their skills as ethnologists, ethnographers, and diplomats. Jefferson had instructed them to learn everything they could about the Indian nations they met and to treat them as friendly as their conduct would permit.

The captains sought to understand Indian languages, diets, religions, locations, enmities, alliances, and customs. They also relied heavily on information and assistance from Indians, without which the Expedition would have failed. The message the captains delivered and the diplomacy they pursued with the Indians focused on establishing intertribal peace and inviting trade with the United States.

The Captains Begin Diplomatic Parleys

Although Clark knew Otos, Missourias and Omahas lived along the river, he postulated that "as those Indians are now out in the praries following & Hunting the buffalow, I fear we will not See them." The party lingered for a few days beginning July 22 at "White Catfish Camp" probably near present Bellevue, Nebraska, to "Send for Some of the Chiefs of that nation [Otos], to let them Know of the Change of Government, The wishes of our Government to Cultivate friendship with them, the Objects of our journy and to present them with a flag and Some Small presents." The captains sent George Drouillard and Pierre Cruzatte west to the Oto village on the Platte, but they found it empty and returned.

The party encountered a Missouria man hunting elk on July 28, and sent him back to the Oto-Missouria camp with Drouillard and La Liberte to arrange for a council. The captains selected a campsite a few miles upriver on the west bank in an area they called "Councile Bluff," near the present site of Fort Calhoun, Nebraska, and Fort Atkinson State Historical Park, and raised their 17-star flag.

There, they opened the Expedition's first diplomatic parley, meeting with members of the Oto-Missouria people – two small tribes who had banded together only about four years before.

At sunset on Thursday, August 2, 1804, Lewis and Clark greeted several tribal leaders and a French trader named Fairfong. The captains gave them some tobacco and some roasted meat for dinner and invited them to a council the following day. The Indians reciprocated with a gift of watermelons. The

KEN BOUC

The Expedition turned out in striking regimental coats, such as this replica of First Sergeant John Ordway's uniform on a few important occasions during the journey, including the July 4th celebration in 1804, at Indian councils, and at Sergeant Floyd's burial.

HIDE TIPIS AT DUSK / CHARLES FRITZ

Sergeant Nathaniel Pryor described the Yankton Sioux tipis to Clark, who wrote: "the Sceouex Camps are handson of a Conic form Covered with Buffalow Roabs Painted different Colours and all Compact & hand Somly arranged, covered all around an orpen part in the Center for the fire with Buffalow roabs each Lodg has a place for Cooking detached . . . " Pryor might have been the first U.S. citizen to see the classic Plains Indian tipi.

captains stayed up late that evening drafting their speech for the morning.

The council opened at midmorning. Lewis and Clark used a mixture of ceremony, diplomacy, promises of trade, and gifts to temper their message of American sovereignty under the Great Father, and to sell the idea of sending a delegation to visit Washington. Clark wrote that they had "Delivered a Speech & made [six] chief[s] gave a fiew preasents and, a Smoke a Dram, Some Powder & Ball[.]" The speech informed "thos Children of ours of the Change which had taken place, the wishes of our government to Cultivate friendship & good understanding, the method of have good advice & Some Directions."

It was important to identify Indian representatives who could speak for the majority of a tribe. Clark sent some presents, along with a medal and a flag, to a high-ranking Oto who was not at the council, and lesser gifts to those attending. Each of them agreed to adhere to the captains' message whereupon Clark gave them 50 musket balls, a canister of powder, and a dram of whiskey.

This 1820 (c.) drawing depicts pronghorns on the Plains. First documented by Lewis and Clark, the pronghorn *(Antilocapra americana)* is the only member of its family in North America and can attain speeds of 70 miles per hour for short distances.

"After Capt Lewis's shooting the airgun a feiw shots (which astonished those nativs) we Set out," Clark wrote in his journal.

The captains had accomplished their objectives – to announce American sovereignty, provide samples of American trading wares, and establish a friendly relationship with the Otos and Missourias. Handing out medals engraved with Jefferson's likeness, passing out American flags and certificates of friendship, exchanging gifts, a "magic show" including magnifying glass, compass, airgun, and a military show of force all became part of the program Lewis and Clark used in other councils along the way.

The councils with the Otos and Missourias were important, but the captains could not make contact with the Omahas. That tribe had suffered a terrible calamity when smallpox swept through its village around 1800, killing Omaha Chief Washinga Saba (Blackbird) and perhaps half of the tribe.

On August 11, the Corps visited the grave of this dynamic and feared Indian leader who had gained power through a combination of effective leadership and the occasional use of arsenic on detractors and rivals. Blackbird was buried in a large mound on a 300-foot-high bluff overlooking the Missouri near present Macy, Nebraska, (see page 34) but the legend that he was buried upright and astride his horse appears to lack credence. The detail of men visiting the grave found a pole on top of the mound holding strings of scalps the chief had taken, and Lewis and Clark added a white flag with a red, white, and blue border to also wave over the chief's grave. A few days later the Expedition passed Ton won tonga, the main Omaha village, which was deserted because the tribe was away hunting.

The Omahas were away, but the captains met with another Oto and Missouria delegation that had arrived, hoping to make peace with the Omahas. These Otos told them of a hill that was always hot on the south bank of the river in present Dixon County, Nebraska. At the site on August 24, Clark recounted that the bluff appeared to have been recently on fire and felt " too hot for a man to bear his hand in the earth at any depth." Settlers later named it the Ionia volcano, although scientists later found that the heat was caused by oxidation of shales within the bluff. The river has since carried the site away.

KEN BOUC

At a re-enactment in South Dakota in 2001, Lewis and Clark historians laid out period replicas of cartographic equipment such as William Clark might have used to make maps during the Expedition. The tools include a sextant, dividers, an inkwell, compass, and magnifying glass.

Nearby, on the other side of the river some distance from the north bank, stood a high, conical hill near present Vermillion, South Dakota. The Indians called this hill Spirit Mound, believing it to be occupied by 18-inch devils in human form. Despite the nearly 90-degree heat on August 25, the captains and nine men set out to verify the veracity of the legend. Seaman, Lewis's dog, collapsed along the way and Lewis labored mightily as well, recently weakened from a near poisoning. When the party ascended the summit, they were rewarded for their nine-mile hike with the spectacular view of the region, but saw no little devils.

Near the mouth of the James River on August 27, three Yankton Sioux approached the party. The captains sent Sergeant Nathaniel Pryor, and Pierre Dorion, Sr., a French boatman, and a trader who had lived among the Yanktons, to invite the chiefs to council. The Corps waited at the base of Calumet Bluff in present Cedar County, Nebraska, just below the spot where Gavins Point Dam now spans the Missouri.

Prophetic Words about the Teton Sioux

Late the next day, Sergeant Pryor, his companions and about 75 Yanktons appeared on the far bank of the river. Clark recorded Pryor's description of the Sioux lodges and village. He wrote "the sceouex Camps are hanson of a Conic form Covered with Buffalow Roabs Painted different Colours and all Compact & hand Somly arranged." Pryor was probably the first U.S. citizen to see and describe the classic Plains Indian tipi and camp.

The Yanktons crossed the river the next day, and the council began about noon. The meeting followed what would become the standard protocol – tobacco smoking, meals, gift exchanges, speeches about American trade and intertribal peace, and a military drill and magic show.

Yankton sub-chief Half Moon delivered a prophetic speech about his Teton Sioux kinsmen upstream. The Yanktons opened their ears to the captains' words of peace, he said, but "I fear those nations above will not open their ears, and you cannot I fear open them."

Later, the captains set the prairie on fire to signal nearby tribes to come to council but to no avail. As with the Omahas, the captains were unable to contact the Poncas, relatives of the Omahas who also had been decimated by smallpox. The Poncas lived in the vicinity of the Niobrara River, but they, too, were away hunting bison on the Plains.

As the Expedition reached the Niobrara River's confluence with the Missouri on September 4, the men noticed a changing landscape. The Expedition was pressing westward onto the dry high plains. Sagebrush *(Artemisia frigida* Willdenow), rabbit brush *(Bigelowia douglasii* Gray), and shortgrass prairie were becoming the

Artist Karl Bodmer depicted the snags in the wild river on his trip up the Missouri in 1833.

The Missouri River Was an Adversary

The Expedition spent two months in what is now the state of Missouri learning what the Missouri River was all about. It was about sandbanks falling in on them, constant battles against strong and shifting currents and eddies, and tree limbs and entire trees charging at them on that swift current. And there was the constant, grueling labor against the river's five-mile-per-hour current, either pulling the keelboat and pirogues with long ropes (cordelling), using the long setting poles, or in some instances wading alongside and pushing.

In the region above the Big Nemaha River, especially near Nebraska's Indian Cave State Park, the Expedition ran into really wild storms. These were violent, quick-moving, summer storms that hit hard with driving rain and high winds before moving on. Getting through all that was difficult.

The river was very wide, much wider than it is today. Channelization now confines the Missouri to a single deep channel. The old, natural river often shifted. The Expedition sometimes had problems with sandbars, on which they often stopped at the end of the day in the middle of the river. On one occasion, the river literally washed a sandbar out from under them in the middle of the night and they were lucky to get to shore. This natural river meandered like a living organism, and it did its own thing. With its meandering, constantly turning left, then right, it was like a snake maneuvering through the grass. The Expedition often had to travel great distances to make a little progress. The most famous example was the Great Bend in central South Dakota, where it was about 22 to 25 miles by water, but a man could get to the same point by walking just 700 meters. Just above Blackbird Hill, the river ran almost 19 miles, a long and difficult day's travel by boat, to get to where a man could walk in 970 paces (see map on page 35).

The river also caused many health problems. The men were drinking muddy, roiling water from the river, and as a result, were constantly battling dysentery. They also had to battle welts and boils under their arms and in their armpits and infected scratches and cuts, the result of being in the river to pull the keelboat and pirogues. Meriwether Lewis, with his rudimentary doctoring skills learned in Philadelphia, used elm bark and corn meal as disinfectants to clean out the boils.

To the men of the Expedition, the Missouri was not just a conduit to get from place to place, but also an adversary. They had tremendous admiration for it, but the river really gave them a lot of problems at times. They had to struggle 1,600 miles through the lower and the middle portions of the Missouri to reach Mandan villages.

– Hal Stearns

norm. Soon, they encountered intriguing animals such as fleet-of-foot goats with keen eyesight (pronghorns) and barking squirrels that burrowed in the prairie (prairie dogs).

As summer faded into fall, the captains may have reflected on the past two months, filled with charting the river, collecting animal and plant specimens and dealing with the party's health problems. They had achieved some success in their councils with the Otos and Yanktons, missed contact with the Omahas and Poncas, and become apprehensive about meeting the powerful Missouri River middlemen, the Teton Sioux.

They had to wonder what awaited them upstream. Would Half Moon's speech prove prophetic, and would the captains regret leaving Pierre Dorion with the Yanktons when he might have helped them in their dealings with the Tetons? Would the Sioux allow them to continue upriver or demand all of their trading goods as a toll, or force them to turn back, or even wipe them out? Would any Indian leaders be willing to travel to see the president? And if they gained safe passage from the Sioux, would they arrive at the Mandan villages before winter blizzards blasted the Plains? Would the animal that the Indians feared, the grizzly bear, pose a threat to this well-armed flotilla? Before they closed their eyes that night, some of the party may have wondered if they would ever see their friend, George Shannon, again.

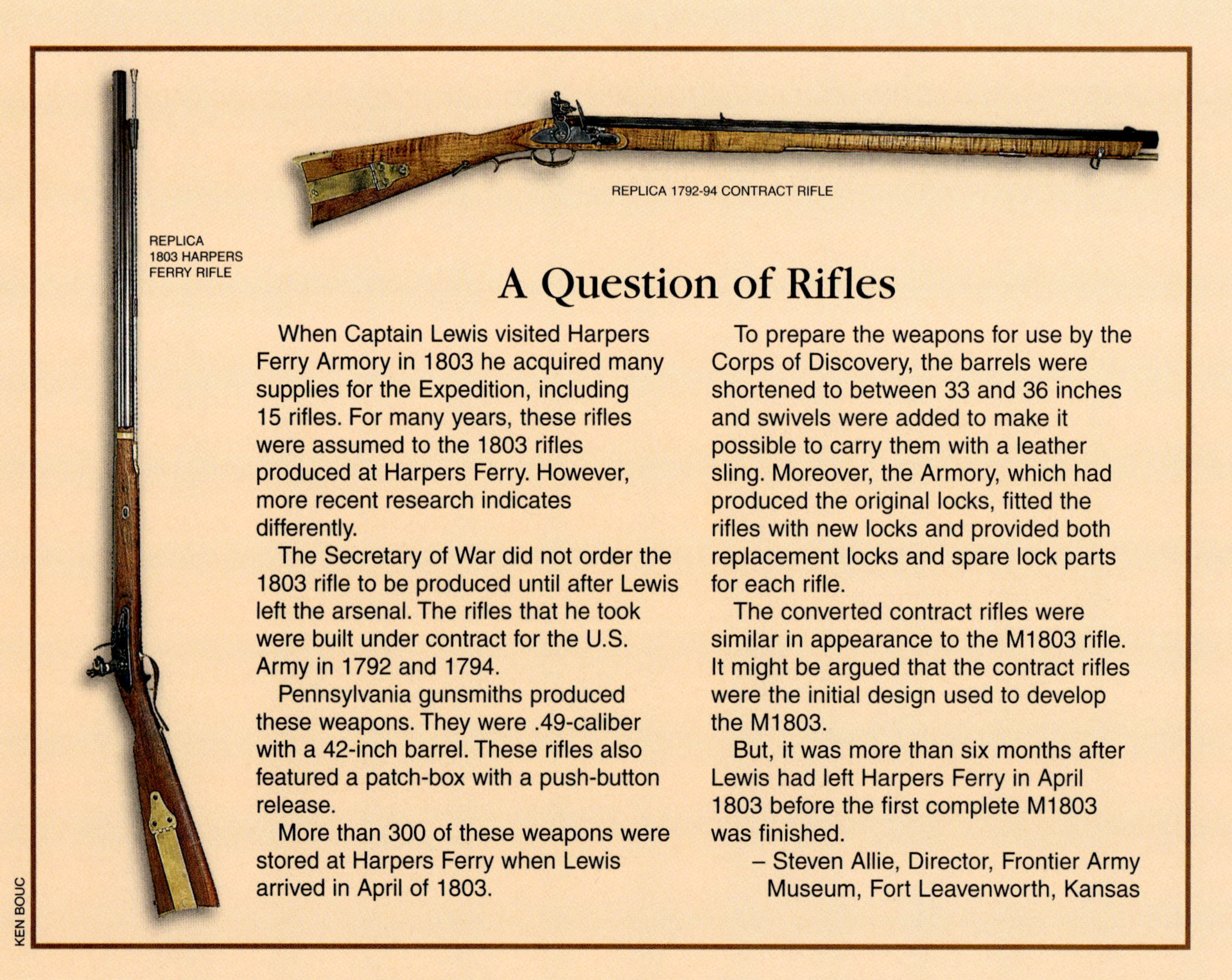

REPLICA 1792-94 CONTRACT RIFLE

REPLICA 1803 HARPERS FERRY RIFLE

KEN BOUC

A Question of Rifles

When Captain Lewis visited Harpers Ferry Armory in 1803 he acquired many supplies for the Expedition, including 15 rifles. For many years, these rifles were assumed to the 1803 rifles produced at Harpers Ferry. However, more recent research indicates differently.

The Secretary of War did not order the 1803 rifle to be produced until after Lewis left the arsenal. The rifles that he took were built under contract for the U.S. Army in 1792 and 1794.

Pennsylvania gunsmiths produced these weapons. They were .49-caliber with a 42-inch barrel. These rifles also featured a patch-box with a push-button release.

More than 300 of these weapons were stored at Harpers Ferry when Lewis arrived in April of 1803.

To prepare the weapons for use by the Corps of Discovery, the barrels were shortened to between 33 and 36 inches and swivels were added to make it possible to carry them with a leather sling. Moreover, the Armory, which had produced the original locks, fitted the rifles with new locks and provided both replacement locks and spare lock parts for each rifle.

The converted contract rifles were similar in appearance to the M1803 rifle. It might be argued that the contract rifles were the initial design used to develop the M1803.

But, it was more than six months after Lewis had left Harpers Ferry in April 1803 before the first complete M1803 was finished.

– Steven Allie, Director, Frontier Army Museum, Fort Leavenworth, Kansas

WAHKTAGELI, YANKTON SIOUX CHIEF / KARL BODMER

Yankton Sioux chief Wahktageli was about 60 years old when Karl Bodmer made this portrait in May 1833. Around his neck hung a large silver peace medal "from the President of the United States." Lewis and Clark were the first to distribute such peace medals to the Yankton Sioux. The Corps held successful councils with the Yankton Indians in August 1804.

Land of the Short Grass

By Ken Rogers

The Niobrara River ushered in the High Plains, with drier air, shorter grass and strange new species. Obstacles loomed, including Teton Sioux bent on tribute, and uncertainty about winter quarters.

SEPTEMBER 1804 WAS A GOOD TIME to be on the Missouri River. Temperatures were moderate, frost had made quick work of the mosquitoes, and elk, pronghorns and deer were abundant. The valley was rich with life and adventure.

President Thomas Jefferson's small band of explorers pushed their boats up the Missouri River, past the wide, sand-clogged mouth of the Niobrara. They entered the High Plains as autumn approached. The landscape changed. Tall grasses, especially Indiangrass and big bluestem, gave way to short, tough prairie grasses such as gramagrass and little bluestem. Fewer and different fruit trees grew. The air became drier.

The cottonwoods began to turn to gold. In the mornings, frost left its mark. Overhead wedges of geese flew south.

Every day, Meriwether Lewis and William Clark worked to shape their men into an expeditionary force, the Corps of Discovery. The skills of every man would be required if the Expedition were to explore the new American territory of Louisiana and find a water route for commerce to the Pacific Ocean.

In St. Louis, the captains had added a crew of French-Indian boatmen to the hunters and soldiers who had wintered together at Camp Dubois, on the Mississippi River at the mouth of the Wood River. There were problems. Not everyone spoke the same language or conformed in the same way to military discipline. The captains needed a close-knit, self-sufficient team.

And before the party could pass into the unknown wilderness, beyond the Mandan Indian villages at the Knife River in present-day North Dakota, at least two serious challenges had to be met. The Expedition's boats had to pass through a Teton Sioux chokehold a few weeks farther up the Missouri. And the captains would have to come to terms with the Mandan Indians, with whom they intended to winter. From the Mandans, Lewis and Clark hoped to get valuable information about the country to the west, beyond the Knife River villages, beyond the edge of their maps made by earlier visitors to the upper Missouri.

North of present-day Lynch, Nebraska, four days after passing the Niobrara

---

Ken Rogers of Mandan, North Dakota, is managing editor of The Bismarck Tribune, *and has studied and written about Lewis and Clark since 1996. Rogers edits, writes and coordinates* The Tribune's *annual Lewis and Clark magazine, which each year presents a different aspect of the Corps of Discovery experience.*

THE NORTHERN LIGHTS / MICHAEL HAYNES

River, the Expedition discovered its first prairie dog town. Journal entries for that day, September 7, 1804, are considered the first scientific descriptions of this curious little animal, part of the naturalistic legacy of the Expedition.

In the days that followed came descriptions of several other notable animals, all from the area that is now South Dakota. These included a pronghorn *(Antilocapra americana)* and a white-tailed jackrabbit (*Lepus townsendi)*, both taken in Lyman County, and later a mule deer (*Odocoileus hemionus*), coyote *(Canis latrans*) and black-billed magpie *(Pica pica)*. In response to Jefferson's instructions to make a thorough record of the plants and animals observed, they would bring information on 178 new plants and 122 species and subspecies of animals unknown to science.

Not all the animals they discovered still roamed the prairies. Clark reported on September 10 the discovery of a petrified backbone 45 feet long with some teeth and ribs still connected. That petrified beast was probably a Plesiosaur, a giant long-necked beast that swam the great inland sea during the age of the dinosaurs.

The next day, the Expedition found George Shannon, whom they had last seen in present-day Dixon County, Nebraska, and who had been lost for 16 days after being sent in search of horses that had strayed. Because he wasn't a good hunter, he went a dozen days with nothing to eat but grapes and one rabbit that he killed. Shannon shot the rabbit using a stick for a bullet because he was out of lead rifle balls.

"Thus a man had like to have Starved to death in a land of Plenty for the want of Bulletes or Something to kill his meat," Clark would later write in wonderment.

While looking for Shannon, the Expedition also had been on alert, watching for signs of the quarrelsome Teton Sioux, who were the largest tribe reported to be on the Missouri and good fighters, too. These Indians had turned back earlier expeditions, so they could control the flow of goods upriver. Jefferson wanted the

During the Expedition, the explorers saw aurora borealis, or the northern lights, several times. (See illustration on page 51). On November 6, 1804, during the construction of Fort Mandan, Clark wrote: "last night late we wer awoke by the Sergeant of the Guard to See a northern light, which was light, [but] not red, and appeared to Darken and Some times nearly obscered, and [divided] many times appeared in light Streeks, and at other times a great Space light & containing floating Collomns which appeared opposite each other & retreat leaveing the lighter Space at no time of the Same appearence."

On September 16, 1804, Lewis wrote that a hunter had killed "a beatiful bird" near present-day Oacoma, South Dakota. It was a black-billed magpie *(Pica pica hudsonia),* and the Corps sent several live magpies to Jefferson in Washington in 1805.

MAGPIE *CORVUS PICA* / TITIAN RAMSAY PEALE

HEAD OF AN ANTELOPE / KARL BODMER

Teton Sioux as American friends and economic allies.

When Clark saw heavy smoke to the southwest on September 23, he knew the Tetons had spotted the Expedition. Then came an incident that set a worrisome tone for what the captains expected to be tough talks with that nation. As Lewis and Clark prepared gifts for the Sioux chiefs, John Colter, a member of the party who had been hunting on horseback along the river, shouted from the bank that Indians, presumably Sioux, had stolen his horse. That put the Expedition on edge.

Five Sioux arrived later that day, wanting to come aboard. They were told that one of their people had stolen a horse, which was to be a gift for the Sioux chief. The captains said there would be no talks or trade until the horse was returned. The Sioux denied taking the horse. Then remarkably, despite his firm nature, Clark backed down and invited the chiefs to council the next day near the mouth of the Bad River, which today is close to Pierre, South Dakota.

From the very start, the council did not go well. The captains learned that their interpreter could barely communicate with the Sioux. They then lavished gifts on one chief, Black Bull, and, in doing so, slighted his rival in tribal affairs, Partisan.

The captains invited three chiefs and four warriors to board the keelboat. They showed the chiefs various items intended to impress them, and everyone drank half a wineglass of whiskey. That's when things began to unravel. The slighted Partisan pretended to be drunk, reeling about the keelboat. The captains decided that Clark would hustle the party of Indians back to the riverbank in a pirogue. It was his intention, Clark wrote in his journal, to reconcile with the chiefs.

Clark's first description of pronghorns was made after he observed them from a distance in present-day Knox County, Nebraska, on September 3, 1804. He wrote, "Several wild Goats Seen in the Plains they are wild & fleet." Nine days later, in what is now South Dakota, Clark killed a pronghorn and both he and Lewis described it detail. Lewis wrote, "I measured the leaps of one which I surprised in the plains . . . and found them 21 feet . . . they appear to run with more ease and bound with greater ability than any anamall I ever saw."

PRAIRIE DOG VILLAGE / WILLIAM JACOB HAYS

The men of the Corps first saw a prairie dog colony in what is now northeastern Nebraska.

Prairie Dogs Bring Expedition to a Halt

On September 7, 1804, just three days after the expedition passed the mouth of the Niobrara River in what is now northeastern Nebraska, the explorers found a colony of curious animals living in a cluster of burrows at the base of 70-foot formation Clark described variously as a "dome," "cone" and a "Cupola." Today, it is called Old Baldy, and anyone in the nearby town of Lynch can tell a visitor how to get there.

Climbing to the top of the Cupola for a view of the river and surrounding area was a typical activity. Soldiers examined the terrain features. Suddenly they discovered a new animal that brought the entire Expedition to an abrupt halt for the day, after just 5½ miles of progress. The Frenchmen called the animal *Petite Chien,* meaning little dog, while Clark at first called it "ground rat" and Lewis referred to it as "barking squirrel." John Ordway gave the animal the name that stuck, "prairie dog." Scientists later gave it a less memorable label, *Cynomys ludovicianus.*

Although they are not related to canines, the prairie dog name is understandable. Clark wrote in the journal that they had a nose like a toy dog, that they would yelp in quick succession like a lap dog, and as they yelped, they would raise their little tails.

Finding prairie dogs was one thing. Collecting them was quite another. Private John Shields shot the first one, which was cooked for the captains' dinner, but it was the last one that would be so easily taken. Having the men lie down near one of the holes and try to grab one when it would pop up just didn't work. So they tried to dig one out, and got down six feet, when they "found by running a pole down that we were not half way to his Lodges," Clark wrote. They also brought some willows up from the riverbank and tried to jab and poke one into leaving his burrow, and that didn't work.

Finally, they formed a water brigade, using every man except the guard posted with the boats and every vessel that they had on the trip to bring water the several hundred yards from the river to the dog town.

Clark wrote, "we por'd into one of the holes 5 barrels of water without filling it." Using the remaining daylight, they were finally able to get enough water up the hill and into the hole to make one solitary, soaked rodent eventually squirm out of the earth and into their hands. This animal was put into a cage and made a pet.

The Corps encountered many more prairie dog towns that fall, and collected more animals so that their skins and skeletons could be preserved as scientific specimens.

The following spring, the keelboat and the return party were sent downriver from winter quarters with a cargo of completed journals, maps, various other documents, Indian artifacts, mineral samples, pressed plants, animal skins and skeletons and other scientific specimens, bound for Jefferson and the scholars in the East.

Also onboard was a live, caged prairie dog, which survived the long journey to Washington. Whether this was the same animal flushed out of its burrow at the foot of Old Baldy is not known. The ever-curious president must have been fascinated.

– Hal Stearns

Instead, as soon as the pirogue reached the riverbank, warriors grabbed the bow rope. Another warrior wrapped his arms around the mast, refusing to leave. And Partisan turned belligerent, saying he had not received enough gifts.

As the situation deteriorated, Clark drew his sword. The warriors, perhaps 100 of them, stood on the riverbank, too close to miss, aimed their arrows and rifles at Clark and the men in the pirogue. Lewis called the men on the keelboat to arms.

Where Jefferson wanted friendship, the Expedition found a charged and potentially violent situation. The fate of the Corps' mission, perhaps its very survival, hung in the balance, just one nervous private, one hotheaded warrior, one accidentally fired musket from disaster. The air might have instantly filled with flying lead and arrows. Clark and the men in the pirogue almost certainly would have been killed and the rest of the party brought under heavy attack.

Travel upriver after a battle with the Sioux would have been unthinkable, and with hundreds of warriors in the area, survival of the rest of the party would have been in doubt. Any exchange of fire would leave a powerful and hostile enemy astride the Missouri, capable of thwarting American attempts at exploration or commerce for many years, and willing to court assistance from British interests to the north.

But before a shot could be fired, Black Bull, the other chief, grabbed the bow rope and ordered the warriors away. Clark's men pushed off the bank and headed back to the keelboat. The Expedition tied up at a nearby island, which Clark named Bad Humor Island for the mood of the day. Clark wrote in his journal, "Their treatment to me was verry rough & I think justified roughness on my part."

The captains were concerned that violence might break out at any time, in part, because there were about 250 warriors in the village and only 41 members in the Expedition.

Clark Wrote, "[we] Suspect they are treacherous..."

The next day tensions eased. The Sioux were conciliatory, and the day ended in a huge celebration with dancing, complimentary speeches and, for the main course, roast dog. It was a friendly evening. The Sioux convinced the Expedition to stay another day, although the captains were leery. Of the incident, Clark wrote: "[We] Suspect they are treacherous and are at all times guarded & on our guard." There came more festivities. Members of the Expedition were offered women by the Sioux, as was often the case with other tribes the explorers encountered. Historian James Ronda in *Lewis and Clark Among the Indians* wrote that Great Plains tribes saw offering sex for goods as an appropriate means of transferring power between individuals and as an honored part of hospitality.

The next night, when Clark was using a pirogue to ferry the two chiefs to the keelboat, the boat struck and broke the keelboat's anchor chain. The craft swung wildly and there was much shouting from the crew, unnerving the Sioux on board, who likely thought they were being attacked. The atmosphere was again tense.

That same night Pierre Cruzatte brought more bad news. Omaha Indian captives inside the Sioux camp warned Cruzatte that the Tetons did not intend to let the Expedition pass. It was the last straw. The next morning, after failing to find the keelboat's anchor, and despite Partisan's warriors again grabbing the bow rope in an attempt to extort more presents, the party of explorers headed upriver with the diplomatic Black Bull aboard.

The Expedition was not home free. The captains had been told another Teton camp was a little farther upriver. The Expedition did not stop there, despite invitations from the Sioux and, once past, the captains set Black Bull ashore. For the next several days the crew stayed alert, worried about an attack from the Sioux that never came.

At the mouth of the Moreau River, now beneath Lake Oahe in South Dakota, Clark saw his first grizzly bear *(Ursus horribilis)* tracks on October 7. It was

BLACK TAILED OR MULE DEER / TITIAN RAMSAY PEALE

Lewis and Clark discovered the mule deer *(Odocoileus hemionus)* when Private John Colter killed one near present-day Oacoma, South Dakota, on September 17, 1804. The captains later gave the species its common name, mule deer, because of its large ears.

Painted in 1833 by Karl Bodmer, these portraits of Sih-Chida and Mahchsi-Karehde show the attire of Mandan Indians in the early-19th century. The Mandans were skillful traders, and in the early-1800s their villages on the Missouri River, in what is now central North Dakota, were an important center of commerce on the northern Plains for Indians and other explorers and traders.

SIH-CHIDA AND MAHCHSI-KAREHDE / KARL BODMER

LEWIS AND CLARK JOURNALS

Lewis drew and described a battle ax on February 5, 1805, while at Fort Mandan. He disapproved of the design because of the short handle, but it was apparently popular among the Mandans. The Corps' blacksmiths made these hatchets and traded them to the Indians for large quantities of corn, an important addition to the soldiers' otherwise all-meat diet.

"verry large," he wrote. Nearby, the Expedition met the Arikara people and Joseph Graveline, who had lived with them for 13 years. The season was passing. On October 9, the weather was so rainy and cold that day the captains didn't even attempt to talk with their hosts.

Later, after successful talks, and with an Arikara chief on board, the party proceeded on, anticipating talks with the Mandans and a winter home. Just before reaching present-day North Dakota, a discipline problem that had been worrying the Expedition came to a head. John Newman had spoken against the captains behind their backs and sown dissension in ranks. He was charged on October 13 with "mutinous expressions" and sentenced to 75 lashes. In addition, Moses Reed, who had earlier tried to desert, was confined with Newman. Both men would be sent back to St. Louis from the Knife River villages.

The notion of flogging the prisoner shocked the Arikara chief. "He thought examples were also necessary & he himself had made them by Death, his nation never whiped even thier Children, from their burth," Clark wrote.

It was mid-October, and the explorers knew the Mandans were not far away. Indian hunting parties were seen, especially those after pronghorns. The swift animals were herded into the waters of the Missouri, where they were vulnerable and easily killed.

Here, Lewis earned another stripe as a naturalist. He found a small bird, apparently in a torpid state. Using a knife, he destroyed its lungs and heart, yet it continued to live for several hours. Lewis theorized that the bird, the common poorwill *(Phalaenoptilus nuttallii),* was hibernating, something zoologists did not confirm until the 1940s.

As the Expedition continued north, temperatures dropped steadily and the leaves fell more rapidly. Using John Evans's 1796 map, the Expedition determined that it was at an abandoned village of the Mandans, near the Chess chi ter River, now the Heart River, just beyond the uppermost reaches of Oahe Reservoir. This had been the center of the Mandan world until 1772, when smallpox reduced their population and made them vulnerable to Sioux raids. Until this epidemic, Mandans numbered more than 10,000. After that catastrophe, the Mandans moved to two villages near the mouth of the Knife River and close to three Hidatsa villages. When Lewis and Clark arrived in 1804, only about 1,200 Mandan Indians remained.

Although individuals with Mandan blood remain today, the tribe was nearly wiped out by smallpox in 1837, when the disease reduced the population to just 138 individuals.

It snowed on October 21, the day the Expedition passed the mouth of the

Challenges Turn Soldiers into Corps of Discovery

The Army often refers to "crawling, walking, and running" stages in the development of a modern soldier, much like the stages of an infant, a toddler and a fully mobile person. The Corps of Discovery was at the crawl stage at Camp Dubois. At this "boot" camp, the men learned about being soldiers and working together as a unit.

The men were typical American soldiers of the time, tough and independent. Many thought nothing of going absent without leave, fighting, cursing, back-talking to the commanders, or giving lip to the sergeants. They didn't realize that one man's discipline and sense of responsibility was of great value to every other man in the group, and that each man relied on the others.

The men's progress was tested early in the journey, on the river in what is now the state of Missouri. But by the time they got to Nebraska, they had progressed to the "walk" stage, although some were still learning the hard way, before a military court.

One of six incidents that resulted in courts-martial occurred near present-day Kansas City. Private John Collins was on guard duty and woke his buddy, Hugh Hall. They sampled the party's whiskey and got quite drunk on the liquor meant to be rationed to the men as a reward or on special occasions such as Fourth of July or Christmas or the captains' birthdays. Both paid a price – 50 lashes for Hall and 100 for Collins. Because Collins had been a problem at Camp Dubois, he received the stiffer sentence.

On July 12, at the mouth of the Big Nemaha River, Private Alexander Willard was convicted of sleeping on guard duty the previous night and sentenced to 100 lashes, the first installment of 25 administered that very night. It is apparent he was still at the "crawl" stage. He didn't understand a soldier must obey orders. If he falls asleep on guard duty, he places the party at risk. His sentence was lenient. The Expedition operated under the Articles of War, which authorized a death sentence for a sleeping sentinel.

The most serious offense of the Expedition was the desertion of Private Moses Reed, who left the party on August 4, 1804 on the pretense of returning to retrieve a knife left at the previous night's camp at the Council Bluff near today's Fort Calhoun, Nebraska. George Drouillard was sent after Reed on August 6, and brought him into camp near Dakota City August 18. Reed was sentenced to four runs through a gauntlet of the entire party of enlisted men, each man wielding nine willow switches. He was also expelled from the military party to work as a laborer. As a deserter, he could have been sentenced to death.

Above Kansas City, and especially in the Nebraska-Iowa stretch, most of the men progressed as soldiers to the "walk" stage, and continued to develop as individual soldiers and as a unit. When they faced the belligerent Teton Sioux, and each man followed orders, did his job, and kept his nerve, they passed the final test as a military unit and advanced again, this time to the "run" stage. After that, most understood that, if they did this together, they could handle the rest of the Expedition; if there was a weak link in the chain, everything would fall apart.

– Hal Stearns

THE MANDAN BUFFALO HUNT DECEMBER 7, 1804 / CHARLES FRITZ

Clark's account of a buffalo hunt on December 7, 1804, reads in part: "the Big White Chief of the 1s Village, Came and informed us that a large Drove of Buffalow was near and his people was wating for us to join them in a Chase Capt. Lewis took 15 men & went out to join the Indians, who were at the time he got up, Killing the Buffalows on Horseback with arrows which they done with great dexterity, his party killed 14 Buffalow, five of which we got to the fort by the assistance of a horse in addition to what the men Packed on their backs . . . those we did not get in was taken by the indians under a Custom which is established amongst them 'i'e. any person Seeing a buffalow lying without an arrow Sticking in him, or Some purticular mark takes possession . . ."

Heart River. Less than a week later, the Expedition reached the Knife River villages, where it was met by the Mandans and Hugh McCracken of the Hudson Bay Company. He was one of a number of traders who visited the villages regularly, coming across the prairie from British territory to the northeast.

The captains presented the Mandans with a cast-iron corn grinder that they had carried upriver from St. Louis. It quickly became clear to the captains that the Mandans would be cooperative hosts, and Clark set about finding a site for a winter camp. Meanwhile, Lewis began making the rounds of the villages, meeting chiefs and pressing for information about the way ahead.

When Lewis left Washington in 1803, the latitude and longitude of three key places in the adventure ahead were known: St. Louis, the mouth of the Columbia River and the Mandan villages near the mouth of the Knife River. There, in a stretch of about six miles, were five villages. The lower two belonged to the Mandans and the Hidatsa lived in the three upriver. It was a significant trade center in the middle of the continent, an early Mall of America. European and native traders came with Spanish horses and silver from the Southwest, and traders based in present-day Canada brought ocean shells and European goods.

Into this trade mix went the corn, beans and squash that the river tribes raised, finished beadwork and Knife River flint, which has also been found in archeological sites as distant as Ohio and New York. Key to this trade network were the skillful Mandan negotiators, who were able to barter with friend and foe.

The Mandans' allies, the Hidatsa, were important to the Expedition as well. Their raiding parties had penetrated as far west as the Rocky Mountains. Several

years earlier one of these raiding parties had captured Sacagawea, a young Shoshone woman who was to prove vital to the Expedition's success. The Hidatsas told the explorers much about the geography to the west.

While the Sioux lived in hide tipis, the Mandans and Hidatsas lived in round earthlodges. Heavy cottonwood beams supported a frame of smaller logs, covered with brush and then earth. Each lodge had a smoke hole in the center.

When Alexander Henry of the North West Company visited the Mandans in 1806 he described a hard-packed, sand-and-clay road between villages with plenty of traffic. There were large fields, worked by women and children, reaching back from the Missouri to the river bluffs. To Henry, it looked like a plantation.

Henry wrote: "The whole view was agreeable, and had more the appearance of a country inhabited by a civilized nation than by a set of savages."

The explorers made friends with two important Mandan chiefs, Sheheke or Big White, and Posecopsahe or Black Cat. It was Sheheke who in 1806 returned to St. Louis and eventually met Jefferson, but Posecopsahe was the Mandan figure who would most impress Lewis.

A site for Fort Mandan was selected on the east bank of the Missouri River, not far downriver from the two Mandan villages. The structure was basically a

EH-TOH'K-PAH-SHE-PEE-SHAH, BLACK MOCCASIN HIDATSA / GEORGE CATLIN

Artist George Catlin found a living link to Lewis and Clark in the early-1830s in Black Moccasin, who recalled the visit of "Long Knife" (Lewis) and "Red Hair" (Clark). Catlin painted this portrait when he visited the Mandans during his journey through the West. Clark told Catlin that he "had considered Black Moccasin quite an old man when they appointed him chief 32 years ago." In the winter of 1804-1805, when the explorers knew him, Black Moccasin was the chief of Metaharta, a Hidatsa village home to Sacagawea and her husband, Toussaint Charbonneau.

compact triangle, with rooms on two sides and the gate on the third. The fort's palisade walls were 18 feet high and would house 40 people for the next four months. Construction began on November 3, the carpenters and their helpers working against time. Winter was approaching. Those not swinging axes to cut trees for the fort spent their time hunting and stockpiling meat for the winter.

As they would to any new prospective trading partner, the Mandans proved to be gracious hosts. When Mandan braves sighted buffalo on the prairie beyond the river bluffs, Sheheke invited the visitors to share in the hunt. It was a cold day, just below zero, and 10 inches of snow covered the ground. Lewis and Clark took 15 men from the Expedition on the hunt. The Mandans on horseback rode among the herd and, using bow and arrows, killed as many cows as they could. That day Lewis killed 14 buffalo, five of which the men hauled to the fort, and the other five going to whoever found the animals, as was the custom. By nightfall, the mercury had fallen to 12 degrees below zero and the river froze over. Three men were badly frostbitten. To stay warm, Clark made himself a cap and lined his gloves with fur from a lynx.

Cannon Volleys Mark Christmas Day

Shortly after the Expedition arrived at the Knife River villages, Toussaint Charbonneau approached the captains. The 46-year-old French-Canadian had been living among the Hidatsa people as an independent fur trader for several years. He offered himself, and, perhaps, his two teen-aged Shoshone wives as interpreters. Lewis knew that he would need horses from the Shoshones when the Expedition reached the headwaters of the Missouri. So Charbonneau and his family took a small hut near the fort and spent most of that winter hunting and working as interpreters for the Expedition.

Charbonneau was a character and a bit of a bungler, at one point later in the Expedition nearly capsizing one of the larger boats out of ineptitude and fear. Clark also chastised him for striking his wife, Sacagawea, who accompanied the Expedition. But he could cook, especially buffalo sausage. And he was a survivor, outliving both Lewis and Clark. With a succession of teen-age Indian wives, he would remain a fixture on the upper Missouri until about 1843.

A steady stream of visitors came to the fort for conversation, food and trade. When the two captains were not entertaining guests or seeking information from them, they were preparing materials to be sent back to Jefferson by keelboat in the spring. Clark worked on his master map and Lewis gathered observations on everything from Indian tribes to botany.

On Christmas Day, the captains asked their neighbors not to visit. Christmas morning, the men fired three rifle and cannon volleys, and the American flag went up on the fort for the first time. The men were given the day off, as well as a ration of brandy. Cruzatte played his fiddle, and the men danced. Then, on New Year's Day, the Expedition traveled from village to village, dancing to Cruzatte's fiddle, entertaining the Indians and celebrating the arrival of 1805.

Clark was dutiful about building a map. He questioned Indians about the country ahead, and he kept extensive notes. Only when a number of sources agreed about where a river entered the Missouri or the distance to a specific geological feature would he finally add it to the map.

Dwindling Meat Supplies Necessitate a Hunt

Indians gave Clark several maps during the course of the Expedition. They might have been drawn in charcoal on hide or shaped in the sand near the evening fire. Clark noted these in his journal, and made copies, the results of which became part of Clark's final map. Sheheke visited Fort Mandan on January 7, 1805, and while there he sketched the country as far west as the Rocky Mountains and south to the Yellowstone Basin.

YORK / CHARLES RUSSELL

Winter truly arrived in January and February with snow and extreme cold, and the wind made it worse. Each of the small cabins in the fort had a fireplace, and keeping them burning took a huge amount of wood. The men were working hard in the cold and needed to eat well to keep going. They required nearly 6,000 calories daily, but meat stocks began to dwindle and much of the game that the hunters brought in was lean. Deer and elk faced the same cold that the Expedition did, burning up their body fat. The men became desperate for meals that contained fat.

Members of the Expedition began to trade with the Indians for corn. Taking apart a sheet-iron stove used on the upriver journey, Private John Shields used a forge constructed inside the small fort to make arrow points and axes. He fired the forge with coals made from burning cottonwood trees. A four-inch square of metal brought in seven to eight gallons of corn.

Indians were intensely interested in York because they had never seen a man with black skin and kinky hair. On March 9, 1805, Le Borgne, a chief of the Hidatsa, visited York in an earthlodge. He spit on his finger and attempted to rub off York's blackness.

WINTER VILLAGE OF THE MINATAREES / KARL BODMER

Hidatsa elders are cloaked in their buffalo robes in a village scene painted in November, 1833. Two young braves practice spearing a hoop on the frozen ground. Lewis and Clark described the domed earthlodges as centers of activity during the winter months. The lodges were heated by a central fire and smoke was vented through a hole in the middle of the lodge roof.

To fill the fort's larders with meat, and hopefully some fat, Clark gathered a party of 16 men from the Expedition and two Frenchmen to backtrack and hunt along the frozen Missouri to the south. The party took two sleds and three horses. Walking on the rough ice bruised and blistered the men's feet and quickly wore out moccasins.

They traveled 22 miles the first day but found nothing worth shooting. After five days of hunting, Clark sent several men and the three horses back to the fort with the best of the meat. Then, he had the men build a wood structure to store the rest of the meat to protect it from scavengers – gray wolves and inky black ravens.

The trip back was easier. The river had broken through and flowed over the rough ice, making a smooth surface. But the loaded sleds were heavy. It took 16 men or one horse to pull a sled. On this hunt, the men killed 40 deer, 19 elk and four bison.

Sacagawea's Vital Role in the Expedition

When the hunting party returned, they were met by the sound of a crying newborn. Sacagawea, Charbonneau's 15-year-old wife, had given birth to her first child, Jean Baptiste. The teenager's labor was difficult. Rene Jessaume, who had lived in the Mandan villages for 15 years before the Expedition arrived, gave Sacagawea a tea made from rattlesnake rattles provided by Lewis. Jean Baptiste Charbonneau, known as Pomp, was born February 11, 1805.

Sacagawea played a large role in the success of the Expedition. As a Shoshone, she spoke the language of the Indians whose horses were essential to the success of the Expedition. When the Corps met the Shoshones, their chief was Cameahwait, Sacagawea's brother. Throughout the remainder of the Expedition, the presence of the young woman and child with the Corps reassured Indian people that it was not a war party.

Sacagawea knew the edible plants, and how to do those things necessary to survive in the wilderness. When the party returned to the Knife River villages, on the return to St. Louis, Clark paid her a tribute in a letter to Toussaint saying she deserved more reward for her efforts than the Expedition could give her.

Game continued to be scarce that winter. When four men went downriver, to pick up the meat Clark stockpiled, they were confronted by a party of 100 Sioux, who stole two of their horses.

Lewis and a group of men tried to go after the Sioux, but were unsuccessful. They did bring back meat from 36 deer and 14 elk, however. Lewis made a big point of pursuing the Sioux for the crime. After all, he had told the Mandan and Hidatsa people that the Americans wanted an end to intertribal warfare, and that the federal government would protect them. But he didn't have the resources at hand to make good on those promises.

The hunting trips were critical to the Expedition because the men lived off the land. Throughout their travels, as well as during the stay at Fort Mandan and the following winter at Fort Clatsop on the Pacific Coast, the men hunted steadily. Raymond Burroughs in *The Natural History of the Lewis and Clark Expedition* calculated the hunters took 1,001 deer, 375 elk, 227 bison, 62 pronghorns, 35 bighorn sheep, 43 grizzly bears, 23 black bears, 113 beavers, 16 otters, 104 geese and brants, 45 ducks and coots, 46 grouse, 9 turkeys, 48 plovers, 18 wolves (only one for food), 190 Indian dogs (bought for food) and 12 horses.

Lewis and the Mandan chief Posecopsahe became friends. On February 8, Lewis wrote: "this man possesses more integrety, firmness, inteligence and perspicuety of mind than any indian I have met with in this quarter, and I think with a little management he may be made a usefull agent in furthering the view of our government." The two men continued to talk throughout the winter.

For some reason, when the Expedition landed at Fort Mandan, their boats were not pulled far enough out of the water, and the keelboat and pirogues froze solid

MAPPING THE MISSOURI – WINTER AFTERNOON AT FT. MANDAN / CHARLES FRITZ

into the ice. The men spent days trying to get them out using chisels, heated stones and boiling water.

From this point, the Expedition would not use the keelboat as it traveled farther west. In the spring, that large vessel would return to St. Louis, delivering specimens and a report for Jefferson. Going upriver required smaller craft. Clark sent 16 men to a stand of cottonwoods upriver to carve six canoes from the huge trees.

The ice on the Missouri began to break up on March 25. With the help of the Mandans and Hidatsas, the Expedition had survived the winter, and it was now time to return to discovery.

An Indian visitor at Fort Mandan traces a map in the snow, showing the explorers the location of an important landmark. Before arriving at Mandan, the explorers had little knowledge about the Missouri River to the west. During the winter of 1804-1805, they sought information from Indians who had followed the river and learned they would encounter a great falls on the Missouri before reaching the mountains.

Of that departure, Lewis wrote: "Our vessels consisted of six small canoes, and two large perogues. This little fleet altho not quite so rispectable as those of Columbus or Capt. Cook were still viewed by us with as much pleasure as those deservedly famed adventurers every beheld theirs; and I dare say with quite as much anxiety for their safety and preservation. we were now about to penetrate a country at least two thousand miles in width, on which the foot of civilized man had never trodden; the good or evil it had in store for us was for experiment yet to determine, and these little vessells contained every article by which we were to expect to subsist or defend ourselves."

Moulton's Journals

By Ken Bouc

The documents of the Lewis and Clark Expedition are a priceless resource. Two decades work at the University of Nebraska has opened these papers to scholars and the reading public.

WHEN MERIWETHER LEWIS AND WILLIAM CLARK returned from their Expedition 40 months after President Thomas Jefferson issued his final instructions, they brought with them small red morocco-bound notebooks containing a record of each day's events. Those journals, along with other volumes of scientific and geographic observations, field notes, maps and military records, constituted the official record of their journey and made it one of history's most thoroughly documented explorations.

Their commander-in-chief had made it clear from the start that he expected a detailed and daily record of their mission, and his captains made sure that he got it. Writing would require extra hours in camp each night, fighting weather, mosquitoes, dim campfire light and the fatigue of the day's labor, but Thomas Jefferson would have his journals.

Today, nearly 200 years later, the story of the Expedition survives in its documents. As treasured historical artifacts carefully preserved in archives in Philadelphia and St. Louis, the little red notebooks and related papers are beyond the reach of most of us. But, Dr. Gary E. Moulton, working just an hour's drive from the Expedition's Missouri River corridor at the University of Nebraska-Lincoln's Center for Great Plains Studies, has changed that.

Moulton and his team have transcribed, studied and interpreted every surviving document of the Expedition. The result of this monumental task, which spanned nearly two decades, is *The Journals of the Lewis and Clark Expedition,* 13 volumes in all. The first, an atlas of the Expedition's charts and maps, was issued in 1983. The last, a comprehensive index of the collection, was published in spring, 2001.

Moulton's widely-acclaimed "Nebraska Edition" is a tremendous advance, providing scholars and serious readers access to the Lewis and Clark papers, according to Stephen Hilliard, interim director of the University of Nebraska Press, publisher of the volumes. "It is a major contribution both to scholarship and the cultural heritage of the nation," he said.

This massive work, with extensive annotation and cross-referencing, obviously caters to scholars and historians. But Moulton and The Press have remembered the general audience as well, according to Hilliard.

Appearing in September, 2002, *The Definitive Journals of Lewis and Clark* is a seven-volume paperback edition limited to the journals written by the captains. *The Lewis and Clark Journals: An American Epic of Discovery,* Moulton's abridgement of his original work, appears in spring 2003. A web site is also being

THE JOURNAL / MICHAEL HAYNES

Sergeant John Ordway writes the days events and his observations in a journal under moonlight and lantern while men of the Corps of Discovery enjoy Pierre Cruzatte's fiddle playing near the campfire.

developed, without a fixed timetable, by The Press, UNL Libraries and the UNL Center for Great Plains Studies.

The foundation of all this is Moulton's 20 years of dedication and scholarship. But the project probably owes its existence to The Press and Steve Cox, one of its former editors, according to Moulton.

Responding in 1977 to growing demand among historians for a new and more complete publication of the Expedition's documents, Cox approached the Center for Great Plains Studies, a body then newly formed at the University of Nebraska-Lincoln and dedicated to a broad approach in the study the Great Plains. The Center decided to take on the project and soon found a co-sponsor in the American Philosophical Society in Philadelphia, the custodian of the bulk of the Corps of Discovery's original documents.

LEWIS AND CLARK JOURNALS

The captains documented their historic trek across the West with precise maps, detailed drawings and rich descriptions of their activities. They told of the people, geology and creatures they encountered along the way and wrote of the scientific discoveries they made. During its epic journey, the Corps of Discovery never ran out of paper, ink or gunpowder. The latter allowed the explorers to live off the land, and the writing materials assured their legacy.

Moulton came from Oklahoma to UNL in 1979 as an experienced editor of historical documents, but not knowing very much about Lewis and Clark.

"I didn't realize the extent of the scientific endeavors in which they were engaged," Moulton said. "My view of Lewis and Clark was the view of most Americans – that it was a romantic adventure, that they were crossing the continent, struggling against the elements, encountering Native Americans that they might have problems with. . . . just making a transcontinental trip."

Thomas Jefferson, however, expected more. He was fascinated by Native American languages and customs and by the sciences, especially botany and zoology. "Lewis was to be his eyes and ears and his recorder and come back with this mass of data to give him," Moulton said.

The scientific nature of the Expedition became quite apparent to Moulton when he began examining the documents. "I thought, 'Oh, no. I've got to edit all of this stuff and explain all of this stuff,' about linguistics, geology, botany, zoology, ichthyology," he said. "I realized that, not only did I have to transcribe this, I had to explain it to a public as ignorant about these things as I. That was the real challenge for me," Moulton said.

Moulton solved the dilemma by using consultants. "Here at the University of Nebraska I already had my experts, right over here across the street. If there was a question about a bird, I called Paul Johnsgard . . . if there was a question about a fish or a plant, I had dozens of those people on City and East Campus and at the Nebraska Game and Parks Commission," he said.

The consultants began their work primarily to help a fellow scholar with his project, but many of them were delighted when they saw the Lewis and Clark material. "They said 'Hey! This is neat stuff,' and got into it beyond pure disinterested academic endeavor. They saw the work of Lewis and Clark, which was really the pioneering work in many of their fields," Moulton said.

The Lewis and Clark journals were first published in 1814, with most scientific material omitted, then again in 1893 with some scientific material added. The text of both 19th-century editions was, however, paraphrased and abbreviated versions of the explorers' writing. In the early 20th century, long-lost documents of the Expedition were being discovered, and scholars were restoring the text as it was originally written to produce more complete and accurate work.

Moulton's approach was to present everything, every fragment of the Corps of Discovery's original papers. Not a single document escaped scrutiny and publication. Moulton included, for example, both the rough draft of daily journal entries, usually done in one notebook, and the finished entry made in another. "The first drafts are important because you sometimes get a slightly different slant on things . . . Even when it was a total repeat, we would put it in so readers could get a sense of not only what was written, but of their method of journal-keeping," Moulton said.

The first volume of Moulton's series, *Atlas of the Lewis and Clark Expedition,* was printed in 1983 in a large format, nearly 14 by 20 inches, to accommodate the Expedition's maps. The maps were primarily the work of William Clark, who was an accomplished surveyor and well-suited to mapping the Expedition's route.

After the Expedition, Clark became Indian agent for the Louisiana Territory. "He kept a big map based on his Expedition map on his wall . . . Fur trappers and traders who had been places Clark hadn't would come by and see him, and he

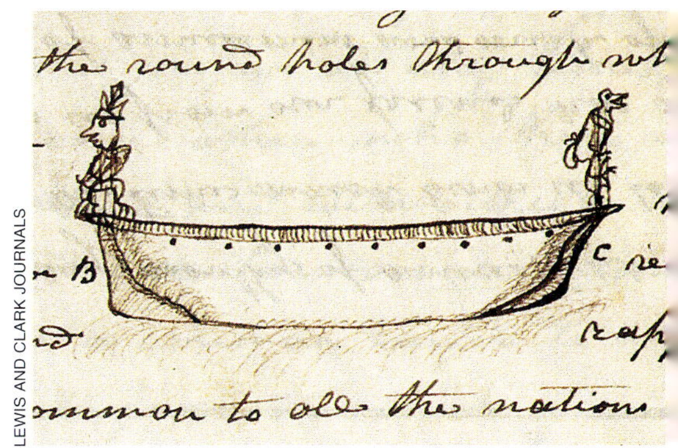

LEWIS AND CLARK JOURNALS

The Clatsop and Chinook tribes of the lower Columbia River were skilled canoe builders. Clark's sketch shows the carved figures that decorated the bows and sterns of many vessels. He was amazed by the Indians' ability to maneuver their craft. On February 1, 1806, he wrote: "I have Seen the nativs near the Coast rideing waves in these Canoes in Safty and appearantly without Concern when I Should it impossible for any vessel of the Same Size to have lived or kept above water a minute. . ."

KEN BOUC

Gary E. Moulton has edited *The Journals of the Lewis and Clark Expedition.*

LEWIS AND CLARK JOURNALS

While in the Pacific Northwest in the winter of 1805-1806, the explorers examined at least two California condors *(Gymnogyps californianus).* Clark described the second specimen in detail in his journal on Sunday, February 16, 1806. He wrote, "I believe this to be the largest Bird of North America. it was not in good order and yet it wayed 25 lbs had it have been so it might very well have weighed 10 lbs more or 35 lbs between the extremities of the wings it measured 9 feet 2 Inches . . ."

would ask them 'what did you see here and here?' and you can see on the original where he made changes and additions," Moulton said. He used this enhanced version of his Expedition map to create a new map of the West (see pages 96-97) which was published in the 1814 edition of the journals. "It was a magnificent map, and it stood as THE map of the West until the 1850s" Moulton said.

For the rest of the volumes, the transcription of original documents was done from microfilm at UNL, mostly by Assistant Editor Tom Dunlay and others. While transcription proceeded, Moulton and his experts would craft the footnotes dealing with scientific and technical aspects of the Expedition. A footnote might pass between Moulton and a consultant several times, being rewritten at each stage. The consultant would concentrate on accuracy, while Moulton worked to make its language consistent and understandable to a general audience.

Occasionally, smudges or faded areas couldn't be read from microfilm, which sent Moulton to the little red notebooks in Philadelphia or St. Louis. "You sometimes had to go to the original, and even there, it could fail you. But most of the journals are still very clean and easy to read," Moulton said.

Besides serving as "a priceless record of the Expedition," the journals also are a valuable tool for continued scientific studies, according to Moulton. Botanists and zoologists today consult Expedition documents and maps for ideas about distribution of plants and animals and the conditions under which Lewis and Clark saw them. And, they learn about changes in climate by comparing carbon 13 in specimens collected by Lewis and Clark and preserved in scientific collections to that in plants growing in the same areas today.

Science was not the only purpose of their mission. Lewis and Clark were extremely anxious to make contact with the people living along their route, hoping to lay the groundwork for future relations between the tribes and the United States. Jefferson had trade in mind, and he hoped to lure them away from the British influence in the north and Spanish influence in the southwest.

Until Lewis and Clark were north of the mouth of the Platte, they didn't meet any natives, primarily because the Indians were on the plains hunting buffalo at the time the Expedition passed through, according to Moulton. The first two encounters – the council with the Otos and Missourias at "councile Bluff" north of Omaha, and the meeting with the Yankton Sioux at Calumet Bluff – were amicable. And in several cases, the Indians they met along the way were not only friendly, but gave the explorers aid vital to their mission or their survival. The Expedition encountered hostility only twice, in a tense shouting match with the Teton Sioux in present South Dakota, and a fight with a party of young Blackfeet in Montana. "The Indian, the human element, was very important," Moulton said.

In working with the journals, Moulton sometimes felt a connection with their authors despite the nearly two centuries that separate them. "Personality does emerge from their language. You see Lewis's personality come out," he said of the more formally educated and eloquent officer, "And Clark less than Lewis . . . Clark is more official, more matter of fact. But that says something about his personality, too, doesn't it?" he said.

Moulton cautioned against reading too much into most of the passages, however. "For the most part, these were not journals that were introspective, personal journals. It wasn't: 'Dear Diary, tonight I feel,' . . . this outpouring of inner feelings. It was an official record of the Expedition. 'We got up this morning. The weather was this. We rowed 40 miles. We saw these animals. We came to and put out the sentinels.' It was an official record," he said, and the enlisted men's journals that have survived are also very direct and to the point.

Yet the journals do convey the sense of wonder that the Corps felt when they discovered something new and truly remarkable. "Both of them (the captains) would comment again and again about the terrain, about the majesty and the awe in which they stood. They would climb up to these heights to get a look at their route ahead, but they would also see the surrounding countryside. Again and again, Clark would use the word 'beautiful', 'beautiful', 'beautiful'," Moulton said. They were struck by the beauty of the plains, according to Moulton, and were not negative about the lack of trees or the dryness as might be expected of someone from the more verdant and well-timbered East.

After some study, the journals also provided an insight into the men that formed the Corps. "You get a sense from the journals of the people in the party who were put on assignments . . . who is the more responsible, who is the more capable . . . The Field brothers, and of course, Drouillard, and Colter . . . These guys have got to be great. Every mission that's important, they're on it," Moulton said.

Perhaps Lewis, more than any of the other journalists, left clues about himself in his writings or, rather, in the lack of them. Although an eloquent writer, Lewis made entries seldom or not at all for extended periods, the longest more than 11 months. "Is this a reflection of his apparent mental instability? Who is to say? There are some good reasons why at some point he wasn't keeping a journal. He may have been doing other sorts of writing, and you can sort of see that in other materials. But in other places there are these gaps that you can't explain," Moulton said. There are many who believe that Lewis did write, and the materials were lost, but Moulton is not convinced. "I believe we have pretty much what was there," he said.

Moulton's work with the Lewis and Clark journals is now completed. "What needs to be done now, and I'm not going to be doing it but other people are, will be the specialized studies. I've already had a graduate student do a dissertation on William Clark, a study of his Indian superintendency . . .We need a really good biography of Sacagawea. What we have is just not adequate . . . We need a good collective biography of what it was like to soldier and serve with Lewis and Clark. That would be a good study, too," he said.

But, as Moulton said, this is work for someone else to do. Opening the journals to others and providing the necessary scientific, geographic and historical interpretation is his contribution to the study of Lewis and Clark, a springboard, of sorts, for other work. In Moulton's words, the documents of the Corps of Discovery are "the record of the Expedition, the raw data from which all the stories and studies of Lewis and Clark come."

LEWIS AND CLARK JOURNALS

During the winter at Fort Clatsop, Lewis mentioned about 100 animals, including some 35 mammals and 50 bird species. Often he wrote with enough precision and detail that the species can be identified today from his words. One example was the greater white-fronted goose *(Anser albifrons)*, which he described on March 15, 1806. With a sketch of the head, he began the description, "There is a third species of brant in the neighourhood of this place which is about the size and much the form of the pided brant [probably an American brant] they weigh about 8½ lbs. . . ."

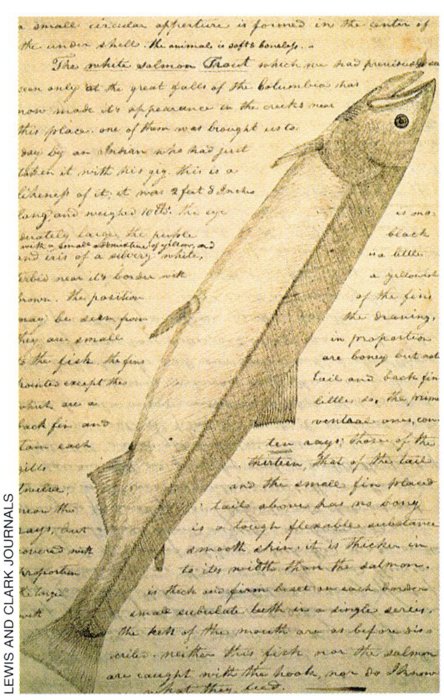

LEWIS AND CLARK JOURNALS

On March 16, 1806, Lewis noted that the "white Salmon Trout" was in creeks near Fort Clatsop. He described the species, a coho salmon *(Oncorhynchus kisutch)*, and drew its likeness.

Stepping Off the Map

By Robert C. Carriker

As the Expedition left Fort Mandan, Lewis noted it entered uncharted country "upon which the foot of civilized man had never trodden." Its greatest perils lay ahead.

WHEN THEY POINTED THE BOWS of their six canoes and two pirogues west again after 163 days at Fort Mandan, the 32 adults in the permanent party of the Lewis and Clark Expedition must have felt a variety of emotions. They wished Godspeed to 18 companions who headed downstream in the keelboat, toward St. Louis. They left friends they had made among the tribesmen at the Knife River villages, and parting was difficult. Nevertheless, shoving off from Fort Mandan at 5 p.m. on Sunday, April 7, 1805, the captains, sergeants, privates, and civilians – including Sacagawea, a Shoshone Indian, and her 55-day-old infant – might have strained their eyes looking west, hoping to catch a glimpse of the unknown they were to explore.

They knew there would be tributaries to the Missouri River, that a great falls would interrupt their progress, and somehow, beyond the Continental Divide, a connection would materialize to send them to the Columbia River and the Pacific Ocean. The prospects before them were both exhilarating and distressing.

For the first few days after its departure, the Expedition experienced nothing unusual. Indian hunting parties came into view, as did French-Canadian fur trappers. The familiar plains environment remained constant and the weather, as expected, brought high winds and cool morning temperatures. The river's current was moderate, mosquitoes were "troublesome," and each day five men penned entries in small journals.

Grizzlies and Bison Attack Explorers

After reaching the Yellowstone River, 19 days beyond Fort Mandan, the environment and challenges to the Corps changed. Fog frequently enveloped the river, and Indians were nowhere to be seen. On 20 occasions, grizzly bears appeared and vigorously resisted the Expedition's entry into their habitat. Another time a bison swam across the river and rumbled into the explorers' camp, nearly stepping on several sleeping men. Some days were more difficult than others. On May 14, high winds came perilously close to capsizing a pirogue. Three

---

Robert Carriker is professor of history at Gonzaga University in Spokane, Washington, where he has taught since 1967. Carriker and his wife, Eleanor, have published on a variety of topics, including the Lewis and Clark Expedition and the Columbia River.

CAPTAIN LEWIS ARRIVING AT THE GREAT FALLS OF THE MISSOURI / CHARLES FRITZ

non-swimmers nearly drowned in the confusion, and only the calm intercession of Sacagawea saved the Expedition's papers, medicine, and instruments.

The river turned nasty, exposing the explorers to the "most considerable rapids which we have yet seen on the missouri." Towlines broke and bare feet slipped in the mud as the canoes struggled against a current that gained power as the river narrowed. After the Musselshell tributary, the plains environment gave way to a series of cliffs and curious landmarks that looked like cathedrals, forts, and rock walls. The explorers felt hemmed in for 10 days.

To gain perspective, Meriwether Lewis climbed out of the Missouri River Breaks. He wrote on May 26: ". . . on arriving to the summit one of the highest points in the neighbourhood I thought myself well repaid for any labour; as from this point I beheld the Rocky Mountains for the first time, . . . these points of the Rocky Mountains were covered with snow and the sun shone on it in such manner as to give me the most plain and satisfactory view. while I viewed these mountains I felt a secret pleasure in finding myself so near the head of the heretofore conceived boundless Missouri; but when I reflected on the difficulties which this snowey barrier would most probably throw in my way to the Pacific, and the sufferings and hardships of myself and party in them, it in some measure counterballanced

Lewis heard the roar and saw clouds of spray from the Great Falls of the Missouri at a distance on June 13, 1805. At about noon, he wrote, "I hurryed down the hill which was about 200 feet high and difficult to access, to gaze on this sublimely grand specticle. I took my position on the top of some rocks about 20 feet high opposite the center of the falls."

Clark's journal entry for July 4, 1805, is titled "Draught of the Falls and Portage." The carefully drawn map shows the Great Falls of the Missouri River and the 18¼-mile route the Corps used to portage approximately seven tons of supplies and equipment. The map is drawn with north to the lower right. The portage took the explorers from June 13 to July 14.

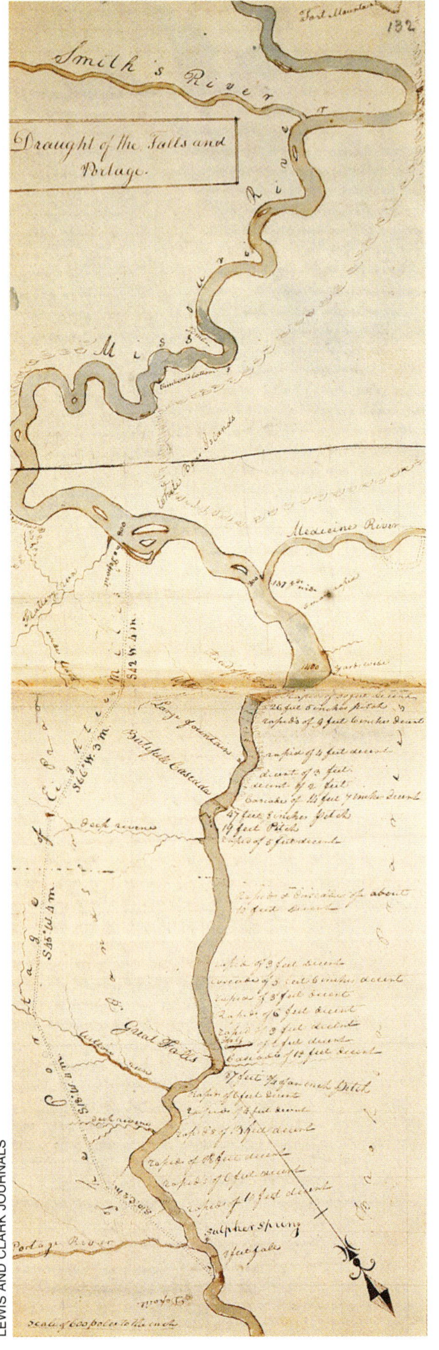

LEWIS AND CLARK JOURNALS

the joy I had felt in the first moments in which I gazed on them . . ."

At the time, Lewis had no idea how right, nor how wrong, he would be.

The Rocky Mountains would, indeed, be covered with snow and give sufferings and hardship to the Expedition, but Lewis was viewing not the main range, only the Little Rocky Mountains. And, ultimately, crossing that barrier would not be the most severe physical trial the explorers would experience before reaching the Pacific Ocean.

Before the Corps of Discovery could test itself against great physical barriers, it first had to decipher a geographical puzzle. When the Expedition arrived at the Marias River on June 2, the men differed over which fork they should follow. Indian informants at Fort Mandan told them to expect tributaries to the Missouri, but counting them and noting the direction of their entry during the actual journey confused the assignment of names given to them by the Hidatsa and Mandans.

FIRST LEG OF THE PORTAGE / RON UKRAINETZ

Which, for example, was truly the "river which scolds at all others?"

Lewis and William Clark spent seven days at the Marias exploring their options. They observed the clarity of the water in both streams, researched the maps in their traveling library, and led reconnaissance units into the field. Then the leaders compared notes, sought the advice of their men, and chose the left branch. Within three days they knew they had made the correct decision when, on June 13, 1805, Lewis and the men in his advance party became the first non-Indians to view the majesty of the Great Falls of the Missouri. Circumventing this barrier would be a major challenge.

The Hidatsa at Fort Mandan had said there would be a falls on the Missouri River, but the Expedition was astonished to locate five falls. Each was magnificent in its wild beauty, and each seemed to be an impossible obstruction. The Expedition would have to portage the falls by establishing two camps, one at

To transport their supplies on the portage around the Great Falls, Lewis wrote on June 17, 1805, "I set six men at work to pepare four sets of truck wheels with couplings, toungs and bodies, that they might either be used without the bodies for transporting our canoes, or with them in transporting our baggage."

THE GRIZZLY ATTACK, MAY 14, 1805 / JOHN F. CLYMER

The explorers had several dangerous encounters with grizzly bears. On May 14, 1805, four men fired simultaneously at a bear and all four hit it, but the bear counterattacked, pursuing the men to the river. Several men attempted to escape in a canoe while others reloaded and fired again. The bear was killed with a shot to the head. The large grizzly had taken eight rounds.

the upper end of the portage trail, and the other at the lower end. The men placed the pirogues, and some of the equipment, in a cache and covered it with dirt. Meanwhile, Clark drew maps and diagrams of the falls for President Thomas Jefferson, and for posterity. Then, the men shouldered approximately seven tons of supplies and equipment and transported it 18¼ miles from one camp to the other. The portage occupied the Corps of Discovery from June 13 to July 14.

The Expedition's time at Great Falls has been called "high drama." Clark called what happened to them "inchantments." Lewis thought "that all the beasts of the neighbourhood had made a league to distroy me," when he recounted a 24-hour period in which he was stalked by a grizzly bear, challenged by a wolverine, charged by a buffalo, and then awoke the next morning to find a coiled rattlesnake

only 10 feet away. On another day, a violent storm pelted the men with baseball-sized hailstones.

There were also moments of profound disappointment. The sinking of the *Experiment,* a portable iron frame boat calculated to hold 8,000 pounds of equipment, topped the list. Covered by elk and buffalo skins, with the seams caulked with charcoal, beeswax, and buffalo-tallow, the boat leaked and had to be discarded. Some of the men might have disagreed, and said the biggest disappointment at Great Falls came on July 4, when the captains distributed whiskey to the men – the last of the 120 gallons they had brought from St. Louis.

The Expedition had seen no Indians since passing the Yellowstone River. Because Indian horses would be essential to cross the Rocky Mountains, Lewis and Clark took turns leading parties overland to seek contact after departing Great Falls. Mosquitoes, gnats, and prickly pear cactus made travel overland especially difficult. There were signs of Indians – abandoned camps, a stray horse, trees stripped of bark, clouds of smoke – and Sacagawea recognized the lay of the land, but there were no Indians. Perhaps the Expedition's armed hunting parties frightened them away.

Traveling overland, Clark and a small party reached the source of the Missouri River while the Expedition's flotilla stayed the course on the river. Above Great Falls 214 miles, the Missouri emerged from an 11-mile wide, untimbered plain framed by two snow-crested mountain ranges. On July 27, the entire Expedition stood at Three Forks, the source of river, and one of the goals set for them by Jefferson.

The topography at Three Forks presented another problem. To choose the correct fork, Lewis climbed a limestone cliff for an overview. This was Sacagawea's homeland, the place where she had been kidnapped as a youth by roaming Hidatsa warriors. With her help, the captains decided that the river they named for Jefferson offered the best chance of reaching the magnificent, shining mountains in the distance. And so, on July 31, after having followed the Missouri about 2,500 miles, the Expedition transferred its energies to a new river.

The boulder-strewn Jefferson River split into three branches five days from the Missouri, then split again. Each time Lewis and Clark had to reconnoiter to find the main stream. On August 8, Sacagawea recognized a landmark known as Beaverhead Rock. As before, Lewis and Clark alternately led advance parties. It was Lewis's party that, on August 11, first encountered an Indian. The Shoshone allowed Lewis to approach to within 100 paces, and then became alarmed and "suddonly turned his horse about, gave him the whip leaped the creek and disappeared in the willow bush in an instant and with him vanished all my hopes of obtaining horses for the preasent." Lewis and his men followed immediately, crossed the Continental Divide at Lemhi Pass on a well-worn trail, and ultimately descended into present-day Idaho. Now the Expedition was in the Oregon Country, not the Louisiana Territory. They were also on Pacific-flowing waters alive with salmon.

Sacagawea Discovers Her Brother

Lewis made contact with the main body of the Lemhi Shoshone tribe on August 13. The chief, Cameahwait, proved to be extremely helpful to the explorers. Overcoming his initial fear that this wandering party of armed men, reinforced as it was by the main party some days later, might be an enemy, Cameahwait assisted the Expedition by transporting their supplies, selling horses to them, and offering information about two possible routes to the salty water. By an incredible circumstance, Sacagawea was Cameahwait's long-lost sister. Her presence further allayed his concerns about the strange white visitors.

Clark found Cameahwait's suggested water route to the west a poor choice after he investigated it. That river, today's Salmon River, had an insurmountable disadvantage. Canyon walls came directly down to the shoreline, making it impossible for a rafting party to either regroup on the bank or climb out of the canyon in an emergency. Unfortunately, Cameahwait's account of the overland route had its drawbacks, too, chief among them being two high mountain passes.

The route was difficult. Even with "old Toby,' a wizened Shoshone as a guide, two more crossings of the Continental Divide – at Lost Trail Pass (6,995 feet) and Lolo Pass (5,233 feet) – consumed most of September and tested the mettle of the men as never before. A confusion of creeks and ravines cut by thickets and high hills obliged the Expedition to cut its own trail at many locations. Horses slipped and fell, some with men on them, some only with packs.

On September 3, the first snow of the season fell in the high mountains, and from that date the Expedition was nearly always cold and wet. It would take until

CAPTAIN LEWIS MEETING THE SHOSHONES / CHARLES RUSSELL

September 22 before the entire Expedition had cleared the mountains and was basking in the sunshine and hospitality of the Nez Perce tribe at their homeland on the Clearwater River. Lewis wrote, "The pleasure I now felt in having tryumphed over the Rockey Mountains and descending once more to a level and fertile country . . . can be more readily conceived than expressed . . . ." The Expedition had passed its second great physical test on its way to the Pacific.

The party spent more than two weeks recuperating among the Nez Perce. Lewis and several of the men were " taken verry unwell," partly from exhaustion, partly from what Private Joseph Whitehouse called "a suddin change of diet [of dried roots and fish] and water as well as the climate." Still, camp work continued. The men branded 38 horses and entrusted them to a chief, they cached unnecessary supplies, hired guides, purchased dogs to eat, and chiseled five dugout canoes from giant ponderosa pine trees.

Leaving the main band of Nez Perce behind at Canoe Camp on October 7, 1805, the Corps of Discovery, for the first time since leaving Camp Dubois on the Mississippi River, paddled with the current instead of pulling against it. They were racing the calendar. Winter came early in these latitudes and they had to

The Corps of Discovery needed to trade for horses and to obtain information about how to cross the Rocky Mountains from the Shoshones. Lewis described finding the tribe on August 13, 1805: ". . . we had marched about 2 miles when we met a party of about 60 warriors mounted on excellent horses who came in nearly full speed, when they arrived I advanced towards them with the flag leaving my gun with the party about 50 paces behid me. the chief and two others . . . advanced and embraced me very affectionately . . . till I was heartily tired of the national hug."

After crossing mountainous terrain, the Expedition dropped down into Ross's Hole in the upper Bitterroot Valley and met the Flathead, or Salish, Indians. After trading for more horses, the party moved down the valley to Lolo Creek and regrouped at Traveler's Rest before going over the Bitterroot Mountains.

reach the Pacific Ocean before they could stop.

The ten-day journey down the Clearwater and Snake rivers, a distance of approximately 250 miles, proved as unnerving to the explorers as had their recent mountain experience. On the Snake River alone the canoes had to navigate 39 rapids and twice the vessels crashed into basalt boulders. Near-accidents were too numerous to record. One rapid extended four miles; another funneled the usual 300-yard width of the river down to 15 yards; and on two successive days the Expedition negotiated nine rapids in 30 miles. "This river in general is very handsome," confided Sergeant Patrick Gass, "except at the rapids, where it is risking both life and property to pass." Sergeant John Ordway thought the rapids comparable to riding in a mill race. Whitehouse believed the current propelled the canoes "Swifter than any horse could run." The captains wished that the Expedition could have portaged around more of the dangerous obstructions, but

the season was "So far advanced and time precious with us."

Reaching the confluence of the Snake and Columbia rivers was both a relief and an enlightenment. Where the two rivers joined a peninsula jutted into the water, and Yakimas and Wanapam Indians shared a village at this location. The excellent fishing and trading opportunities at the junction encouraged Umatilla, Walula, Palouse, and Nez Perce bands to visit on a regular basis.

For two nights and a day the Expedition paused there to celebrate the moment, for they had achieved another of Jefferson's principal goals, reaching the Columbia by an overland route. Lewis and Clark measured the rivers – the Columbia was 960 yards wide – made observations to calculate longitude and latitude, and familiarized themselves with the habits and culture of the Indians who lived on the Columbia Plateau. But the clock was ticking toward winter. Reluctantly, they moved on.

LEWIS AND CLARK IN THE BITTERROOTS, SEPTEMBER 16, 1805 / JOHN F. CLYMER

The Expedition endured an 11-day forced march in September 1805, part of the time in deep snow, to cross the Bitterroot Mountains in what is now Idaho. With no hope of finding game and pushed to their physical limits, the men killed and ate three colts to survive.

When they left the juncture of the Snake and Columbia rivers, Lewis and Clark did not know that only 325 miles separated them from the Pacific Ocean, but they saw clues as they got closer and closer. On October 18, Clark saw a "conical form covered with snow" which he called Timm Mountain, but soon came to realize was Mount Hood. Similarly, on October 19, Clark observed what he thought to be Mount St. Helens, but, in reality, was Mount Adams.

Clark knew from his pre-Expedition preparation that a 1792 Royal British Navy Expedition had named several prominent Cascade Mountain peaks when it journeyed 100 miles up the Columbia from the Pacific. Clark understood that when he reached either of those mountains he would be within a hundred miles of the ocean. In addition, the Indians they met wore some European clothing and used forged knives, obvious signs of a continuing trade with Europeans and

Americans at the mouth of the Columbia River.

These pieces of good news, unfortunately, were tempered by a deteriorating relationship with the Indians. Only two days after transferring from the Snake River to the Columbia, the Expedition entered a zone of rapid water. By October 22, the river began to include falls and chutes, barriers impossible to negotiate in canoes loaded to the gunwales with tons of supplies. The Expedition got help from the natives when they portaged around the obstructions, but relations between the two groups became strained. Impatient to reach the ocean, the explorers spent less time than before trying to understand cultural attitudes of the Columbia River tribes, and soon the Expedition and Indians shunned one another.

The Corps navigated successfully through the Columbia Gorge by November 1, leaving behind a turbulent relationship with the native people. For a week the Columbia's flow was placid, although the current remained strong. On November 7, just a month after the Expedition took to the water at the Nez Perce Canoe Camp, the explorers caught sight of the Pacific Ocean: "Great joy in camp we are in View of the Ocian," Clark wrote.

Joy turned quickly to desperation. Pounding surf in the five-mile wide estuary of the powerful Columbia River nearly beat the men senseless.

To travel the Clearwater, Snake and Columbia rivers to the Pacific, the Corps cut down Ponderosa pines large enough to burn and hew out five crude canoes. In these unstable craft, the party headed downriver on October 7, 1805, and encountered many dangerous rapids along the way. In one short stretch the roaring river dropped 38 feet through a narrow passage between cliffs rising nearly 3,000 feet.

AGAINST THE ODDS / LOUIS ARCHAMBAULT

CLARKIA PULCHELLA / FREDERICK PURSH

Lewis collected some 240 plant specimens during the Expedition. One was ragged robin, formally named *Clarkia pulchella* eight years later by botanist Frederick Pursh to honor Clark. Lewis found the plant, which was new to science, on June 1, 1806, in the Clearwater River Valley, and he described it in his journal with great detail.

Thunderstorms pelted the Expedition and, worse, loose rocks and mud tumbled down from the heights above. The explorers made four camps in eight days on the north shore of the estuary, each time seeking refuge from waves that hurled giant tree trunks at the beach. But even from these threatened camps the captains went about their work.

First, it was important for the Corps to cross the headlands to touch the ocean. Next the Expedition established a relationship with the coastal Indian tribes. Then, when all in the Expedition agreed they had completed their journey, Clark set up his equipment and took longitude and latitude readings so that the president, and all others who would read their journals, might know of their accomplishment.

The Expedition chose to remain at the estuary during the winter of 1805-1806. On November 26, the men relocated to the south side of the estuary where coastal mountains would shelter them from both the "river roaring," and the Pacific Ocean, which Clark coyly continued to call the Great Western Ocean inasmuch as "I have not Seen one pacific day Since my arrival in its vicinity . . ."

The Corps commenced building its winter residence on December 7, and named the structure Fort Clatsop after a local tribe. The month that the explorers spent unsheltered at the mouth of the Columbia River was probably the greatest

THE SALTMAKERS, JANUARY 5, 1806 / JOHN F. CLYMER

challenge faced by the men of the Lewis and Clark Expedition during their entire 8,000-mile journey.

The men passed time at Fort Clatsop in various ways. They hunted elk, repaired clothing, and boiled salt out of ocean water at the beach. Everyone stayed out of the rain as much as possible. Clark estimated that there were only a dozen days between November 4, 1805 and March 23, 1806 without rain, and the sun shone only on six days.

The Captains Make a Bold Plan

Holidays, such as Christmas and New Year's Day, did not mean much in the wilderness. The anticipation of encountering one of the fur trade ships that frequented the mouth of the Columbia did matter, but the enlisted men of the Expedition never saw a sail on the horizon.

Lewis collected and described for science nearly three dozen local plant species, showing a special interest in the large trees of the region. He also identified one hundred animals native to the lower Columbia. His observations about local Indian food, clothing, homes, and weapons later proved invaluable to ethnographers. His most important activity, however, was the rewriting of 179 pages of the

During the winter of 1805-1806 while at Fort Clatsop, the Corps set up a salt-making camp on the beach. The men extracted salt by boiling seawater and then scraping the salt residue from the sides of the kettles. On January 5, 1806, Lewis wrote: "We found it excellent, fine, strong, & white. This was a great treat to myself and most of the party. . . . I say most of the party, for my friend Capt. Clark declares it to be a mear matter of indifference with him whether he uses it or not; for myself I must confess I felt a considerable inconvenience from the want of it."

Expedition journals. Meanwhile, Clark occupied himself reworking his master map of their route since leaving Fort Mandan.

From these efforts, Clark and Lewis formed a bold plan for their return journey. They would split into units. Lewis would explore a shortcut between the Lolo Trail and Great Falls, a route that several tribes had made vague reference to on the route west. This would also be an opportunity to test the northern extent of the Marias River. Simultaneously, Clark would locate the Yellowstone River in the Rocky Mountains and follow it to its junction with the Missouri. This could be a dangerous plan, even foolhardy, but so anxious were Lewis and Clark to test their hypotheses that they pushed forward the date for the return journey to March 23, 1806.

Paddling against the current of the Columbia River turned out to be the easy part of the first leg of the Expedition's return journey. Portaging three large and two small canoes around rapids and over falls during the river's spring runoff was a more trying assignment because the river ran 12 feet higher in spring than the previous fall. And, it seemed, the more the Expedition needed help, the less enthusiasm the local tribesmen exhibited. To remedy this problem, the explorers sold their canoes at the earliest opportunity and traded everything they could spare, including pots, ammunition, and uniform clothing, for packhorses. When they had acquired 23 horses the Expedition headed overland using an ancient Indian trail, thereby cutting off 150 miles of Columbia and Snake River rapids. Upon their arrival at the Nez Perce camps on May 8, 1806, the Expedition received the same warm welcome as they had experienced the previous September when, cold and nearly starved, they stumbled out of the Bitterroot Mountains.

MIMULUS LEWISII / FREDERICK PURSH

Lewis's monkey flower *(Mimulus lewisii)* was another plant that Frederick Pursh acknowledged as a species new to science found on the Expedition.

For 27 days the Corps enjoyed the company of the Nez Perce Indians at a place they called Camp Chopunnish. The camaraderie seemed more like that at Fort Mandan than the undercurrent of hostility of Fort Clatsop. The men learned from their Nez Perce comrades, for example, how to geld horses Indian-style and the technique for steam cooking bear meat over pine boughs. Food was a constant problem, not only for the Expedition, but also for the Indians. At Fort Mandan the Expedition had gained some food with the skills of the company blacksmith; at Camp Chopunnish the Corps relied upon the "medical practice" of Clark to supplement the larder.

Going east across the snow-clogged Lolo Trail in June of 1806 was only slightly less difficult than going west the previous September. Their first attempt to stay on the ancient trail ended in failure as the horses floundered in snowdrifts twice the height of the men. Fear of becoming lost in the mountains forced a halt, a retreat, a regrouping, and later, a second assault on the mountains.

Hired Indian guides helped the Corps find a route and all arrived safely on the east slope of Lolo pass. Clark wrote: "Descended the mountain to Travelers rest leaveing these tremendious mountains behind us, in passing of which we have experienced cold and hunger of which I shall ever remember . . ."

On July 3, after a few days rest, the Expedition embarked upon the great adventure of their return journey. At Fort Clatsop they had decided to divide into two groups. From Clark's map, they probably were able to estimate their designated assembly point, where the Missouri and Yellowstone rivers join, was about 500 miles away. But they could not have guessed how many miles each party would actually travel to get there because both Lewis and Clark were taking new routes to the rendezvous. Nor could they have anticipated that they would be separated from each other for 40 days. Nevertheless, the captains and their parties went their separate ways from Traveler's Rest on July 3 after exchanging warm good-byes and good wishes.

Clark moved on with 23 members of the Expedition riding 50 horses. His route took him down the familiar Bitterroot Valley. From there, he got creative. Instead of using Lost Trail Pass, which they had followed the previous August, he diverted to another, less rigorous, pass used by the Flathead Indians. This put his party into the Big Hole River Valley, another new experience. Sacagawea recognized

SACAJAWEA AT THE BIG WATER / JOHN F. CLYMER

Sacagawea Explores the Big Water

Walking on the Pacific Ocean beach was perhaps the most unexpected and memorable event in the life of Sacagawea, the Shoshone woman who accompanied the Lewis and Clark Expedition. The vast Oregon beach, with its never-ending wave action, was simply fascinating to the 16-year-old, who had lived her entire life in the Rocky Mountains and Great Plains. Nothing in her past to that day, January 7, 1806, had prepared her for such a compelling experience.

During the previous eight months, Sacagawea had had many exhilarating moments – references to her appear 114 times in the Expedition journals – but wading ankle-deep into the surf of the Pacific Ocean must have been wonderful.

Sacagawea, a Shoshone of the Lemhi band, lost contact with her family at the age of 12, in about 1800, when a raiding party of Hidatsa warriors kidnapped her at the Three Forks of the Missouri. In time, she was taken to the Hidatsa village at the Knife River and it was here that she became a common-law wife of French-Canadian fur trader Toussaint Chabonneau.

When Lewis and Clark hired Charbonneau as an interpreter in 1804, Sacagawea accompanied him and also served as a linguist for the Corps. Her translation in the presence of her brother, now the chief of the Shoshone tribe and the possessor of many horses needed by Lewis and Clark to traverse the mountains between the Missouri and Columbia rivers, was indispensable. On other occasions, Sacagawea provided the explorers with information about natural foods and several times she recognized landmarks, but most important was her presence with her infant son, Jean Baptiste Charbonneau. William Clark wrote, she "reconciles all the Indians, as to our friendly intentions."

So, when this stalwart member of the Expedition asked for a favor, no considerate captain could refuse. After Clark announced his intention to view a beached whale south of Fort Clatsop, Lewis noted that ". . . the Indian woman was very impotunate to be permited to go, and was therefore indulged; she observed that she had traveled a long way with us to see the great waters, and that now that monstrous fish was also to be seen, she thought it very hard she could not be permitted to see either." She never forgot participating in this five-day journey, along with 14 others. In addition to walking on the beach, the party cut across the top of Tillamook Head, an exhausting journey whose one compensation was that from the summit, Clark wrote, "I beheld the grandest and most pleasing prospectus which, my eyes ever surveyed, in my frount a boundless Ocean; to the N. and N.E. the coast as far as my sight Could be extended, the Seas rageing with emence waves and brakeing with great force . . ." In addition, Sacagawea witnessed the technique of the Indians as they rendered whale blubber into oil, several gallons of which the Corps purchased. Clark thanked "providence for directing the whale to us; and think him much more kind to us than he was to jonah, having Sent this monster to be Swallowed by us in Sted of Swallowing of us as jonah's did."

Lewis and Clark wrote Sacagawea's name 23 times, spelled 15 different ways, and each of them used the hard "g" sound in the third syllable. An alternative spelling with a "j" (Sacajawea), originated in 1814, with the first publication of the journals, but declined in usage with the advent of modern scholarship.

Little is known of her life after her return to Mandan. The best evidence is that she died at Manuel Lisa's trading post on the Missouri River in South Dakota in 1812.

Her son was educated by Clark in St. Louis, beginning at about age six. He traveled in Europe for six years from 1823 to 1829. When he returned the United States, he became a mountain man, fur trader and guide and ultimately settled in California. He died in 1866.

– Robert Carriker

portions of the area and soon everyone was back on track at the location where the Expedition had met the Shoshones on the way west.

Six of seven cached canoes were recovered and taken to Three Forks of the Missouri River. At this point, Ordway and nine men took responsibility for bringing the canoes downstream to Great Falls where they would rejoin Lewis. Meanwhile, Clark and the rest of his unit kept the horses and went in search of the Yellowstone River, which they found at the eastern end of a pass pointed out by Sacagawea.

Because the Yellowstone flowed fast and free, Clark stopped to hollow out two 28-foot canoes to speed his journey. While the party stopped to build the canoes, two dozen horses disappeared one night. Undeterred, Clark continued on with part of his group in the canoes, traveling about 60 to 75 miles per day in the spring flow. He left Sergeant Nathaniel Pryor in charge of a detachment herding the remaining horses. However, Pryor's party lost the rest of the horses, and took

LOUISIANA TANAGER CLARK'S CROW LEWIS'S WOODPECKER / ALEXANDER WILSON

After the Expedition, Lewis went to Philadelphia and while there asked noted bird artist Alexander Wilson to make portraits of specimens that Lewis had collected in the West. Wilson made drawings of three birds and named each species. They are (clockwise from upper right) Lewis's woodpecker *(Melanerpes lewis),* Clark's crow, now Clark's nutcracker, *(Nucifraga columbiana),* and the Louisiana, now western, tanager *(Piranga ludoviciana).*

FORT CLATSOP / JOHN F. CLYMER

The Corps built Fort Clatsop, which was about 50-feet square with two structures inside, over a three-week period in December 1805. The Clatsop and Chinook Indians traded with the Expedition during daylight hours, but the fort was secured at night. Because of their illnesses, poor diet and the rainy weather, many of the explorers considered their winter at the fort a miserable period.

time to build two seven-foot buffalo skin Mandan-style boats for his transportation. As a result, Clark and his detachment reached the Missouri first, on August 3, traveling an estimated 837 miles from Three Forks, and Pryor's party arrived five days later. Because Lewis and the others did not appear at the confluence by August 9, Clark moved slowly down the Missouri for a few days to keep the men active and the Corps in motion.

Lewis, meanwhile, conducted his own reconnaissance. He took nine men, five Nez Perce guides, and 17 horses north from Traveler's Rest. When they reached the clear path of what the guides called "River of the Road to Buffalo," the Indians took their leave and Lewis and his men proceeded.

When the men reached a broad pass across the mountains and could see the plains adjacent to the Great Falls of the Missouri, they knew all was well. On July 11, 1806, Lewis and his party stood on the banks of the Missouri River in the vicinity of Great Falls just opposite the portage camp where they had spent the night of July 14, 1805.

Though he barely believed it at the moment, Lewis had just taken only eight days to move between the base of Lolo Pass and Great Falls, a journey that was 49 days and 600 miles shorter than the route the Expedition followed in the summer of 1805. Such calculations took time, and Lewis had important work to do if he wished to meet Clark at the Yellowstone River.

The cache of goods left at Great Falls had to be unearthed. And the wheels used to transport canoes in 1805 needed reconditioning so that when Ordway arrived with the canoes they could be transported around that "sublimely grand object" – the falls. It should take eight days when Ordway arrived, Lewis calculated. Lewis placed Gass in charge of the details so that he, Joseph and Reubin Field, and George Drouillard could explore the Marias River. Lewis and Gass agreed to meet on August 5 at the confluence of the Marias and Missouri rivers.

The Marias would include the northernmost point of the Louisiana Territory, Lewis reasoned, and he hoped to determine its latitude and longitude. Ten days after setting out, within sight of the continental divide in present Glacier National Park, he saw Cutbank Creek, the Marias northern tributary, emerge from the mountains to the southwest. They had reached the northern-most point of the river. Unable to take celestial readings because of clouds, the party turned back.

The Marias River exploration became precarious on July 26 when Lewis spied in the distance "a very unpleasant sight" of eight mounted Indians intently watching Drouillard as he hunted along a river nearby. Lewis, resolved to die fighting if necessary, approached the Indians.

Alarmed, but not afraid, the Indians agreed to a parley, which lasted so long that the Indians and explorers shared a campsite that evening. In the morning, an early-rising Blackfeet Indian grabbed away the guns of two Expedition members, and a melee ensued. Two Blackfeet died, one by Lewis's bullet and the other by Reubin Field's knife, but their kinsmen escaped, probably to bring reinforcements.

The explorers rode just as hastily in the opposite direction, toward the rendezvous with the men with Gass and, they hoped, Ordway. From dawn to dawn, Lewis and his men spent 20 hours in the saddle riding perhaps 100 miles. Miraculously, in another dozen miles the beleaguered men saw the six dugout canoes of Gass and Ordway just coming into view.

The Explorers Reunite on the Missouri

Quickly, they released the horses, dug up some supplies left the previous year, and took to the water for 15 miles before stopping in comparative safety for the night. From the Marias to their meeting with Clark, Lewis and his group concentrated on speed. Everything else seemed trivial. Lewis caught up with Clark on August 12.

The great gamble had worked. They had split the command into five units for six weeks, and managed to keep everyone alive – but only by the narrowest of margins. Clark's command weathered several attacks by swimming grizzly bears, and by wolves, who penetrated the perimeter of the camps, and a leg wound to one of the men that incapacitated him for two weeks.

Drouillard and the Field brothers told of their encounter, alongside Lewis, with the Blackfeet. Lewis was injured when he rejoined Clark, the result of being shot in the buttocks, most likely by Pierre Cruzatte, in a hunting accident on August 11. Lewis confided to his journal that he had the "pleasure of finding them all well" at the reunion, and then he ceased writing in his book forever.

Clark could take them the rest of the way home. Injured and still reflecting on his flirtations with death, Lewis remained in the background during the remaining 43 days of the journey.

Two days after the reunion, the Knife River villages of the Mandan and Hidatsa came into view and the Corps of Discovery was back on the map. As early as August 11, two fur traders from Illinois had made contact with the Expedition, and there would be many more such encounters the rest of the way to St. Louis.

Tying up loose ends at the Mandan village took some time. John Colter asked for and was granted an early release from his commitment, Indian chiefs and their families were recruited for all-expense paid visits to the seat of the federal government in Washington, D.C., and equipment no longer needed was given to the Indians. The men of the Expedition said good-byes to Toussaint Charbonneau (who was paid $500 for his services), Sacagawea, and their child, Jean Baptiste, nicknamed "Pomp." Then it was time to go.

On August 17, 1806, the Corps loaded canoes and began a hell-bent dash to St. Louis. Often 50 miles of Missouri River channel passed beneath them from sunup to sundown. Clark estimated that he saw 20,000 buffalo on the plains during one day, but it was porcupine for dinner because they, along with wild

HOMEWARD BOUND / ROBERT F. MORGAN

plums, took less time to acquire. At one point the men covered the same distance in 15 days that had taken them 51 days on the upstream route two years earlier.

Buying chocolate and whiskey from the outward-bound fur traders encouraged the men of the Corps to stay in the canoes longer each day. One area of the Missouri River that the Expedition considered to be dangerous navigation on June 15, 1804, did not alarm them in the slightest on September 17, 1806. When Clark calculated that the Expedition was only 140 miles from "the settlements," the men decided to divide that distance into just two days of hard paddling, even though some of the men suffered from a "singular disorder" of sore eyes.

But sore eyes quickly became well when, on September 20, the men saw the village of La Charette, and the next day St. Charles, and the day after that St. Louis, each of which welcomed the returning explorers with huzzahs of approval from the shore.

The men in the canoes responded with gunshots of joy. They would no longer need to conserve their powder and ball for defense against the unknown. For them there were no unknowns. They had seen an 8,000-mile frontier, and they had conquered it in 28 months.

When reaching present-day Montana on their return trip, Lewis and Clark divided their party to widen their explorations. On July 13, 1806, Clark's group reached Three Forks on the Missouri River and Clark split his party again. Robert Morgan's painting depicts Clark sending Sergeant John Ordway and nine men in cottonwood canoes north to meet Lewis's group at the Great Falls. Clark and his remaining party traveled east in search of the Yellowstone River. The Expedition reassembled east of the convergence of the Yellowstone and Missouri rivers on August 12.

Remote Trail Sites

By Robert C. Carriker

Two of the most remote and beautiful stretches of the Lewis and Clark trail that can still be followed today are in Idaho. The men of the Corps of Discovery traversed both during their return journey in 1806.

ROBERT C. CARRIKER

The best way to explore the possible routes that Sergeant John Ordway took in late-May 1806 is to take a raft down the Salmon River in Idaho.

Salmon River, Idaho

On the return journey, for six weeks in May and June in 1806, the Lewis and Clark Expedition lived among the Nez Perce Indians and waited for the snow on the Lolo Trail to melt enough to allow safe passage.

During their stay, food supplies dwindled to the point that the captains, on May 27, ordered Sergeant John Ordway and two men of his choosing into the field to search for salmon.

Ordway proceeded overland for some miles, then dropped down a steep bluff to a river, which he thought to have been earlier named for William Clark. Disappointed that there were no fish to be caught or traded for, Ordway retraced his steps to the summit of the bluffs, continued west, and followed a second path more than 2,000 feet down to another river, which he believed to have been earlier named for Meriwether Lewis.

With little success again, Ordway rejoined the captains on June 2 with only 17 salmon to show for his efforts. But he had an amazing geographical story to recount.

Ordway's, Lewis's and Clark's journal entries for this Expedition are clouded with uncertainties. Ordway's route from present Kamiah, Idaho, to either Maloney Creek or Deer Creek, which he took down to today's Salmon River, is in dispute; the path he followed to the Snake River is equally debatable.

Today, historical investigation of the location of Ordway's river intercepts form the greatest "what-if" possibilities on the entire route of the Corps of Discovery.

The Hungery Creek drainage in Idaho's Bitterroot Mountains is still one of the most inaccessible stretches of the entire Lewis and Clark trail. On June 17, 1806, the Expedition stalled in this valley.

The best way to form your own theory is to take a raft down the Salmon River and explore Maloney Creek and Deer Creek. Then continue on to the Hells Canyon of the Snake River and consider the possibilities of an ancient fishery at Wild Goose rapids.

Many modern-day explorers follow the well-known trail of Lewis and Clark. But only the most intrepid of latter-day adventurers follow the less well-marked trail of Sergeant Ordway.

Hungery Creek, Bitterroot Mountains, Idaho

Sharing a camp with the Nez Perce Indians on the Clearwater River at present-day Kamiah, Idaho, in May and June of 1806, the Corps was within sight of the Bitterroot Mountains.

The Expedition's first crossing of the Bitterroots, when going west in September 1805, had been a 99-mile endurance test in rough, steep terrain at elevations above 7,000 feet with deep snow. The men were cold, wet, and hungry.

History repeated itself on June 15, 1806, when the Expedition tried to cross the Bitterroot Mountains in present-day Idaho by following a Nez Perce path called the Lolo Trail.

The men and their pack train of horses traveled 22 miles up a gradual incline on the first day. The next day, the grass ran out and the snow – as deep as ten feet – accumulated. The men camped next to a deep, swift creek, an omen of what was to come.

On June 17, the trail narrowed appreciably, so much so that the Expedition twice crossed over in spite of the great risk to men and animals.

Eventually the party moved above the drainage, but the snow became so deep and the trail so vague the captains stopped for two hours to discuss "what was best to be done." At 1 p.m. Lewis writes that "we began our retrograde march. . . We returned by the rout we had come to hungry creek, which we ascended about 2 miles and encamped." Not until nine days later did the Expedition resume its journey on the Lolo Trail.

Today Lewis's "hungry creek" is named Hungery Creek and is one of the most inaccessible stretches of the entire Lewis and Clark trail. Even in perfect weather conditions, a hike along the trail is exceptionally rugged because the natural vegetation is close, stifling, and often impenetrable

U.S. Forest Service officers often ask hikers who are beginning the ascent along Hungery Creek, "Do you have the legs for it?" Those who don't usually experience what Lewis called a "retrograde march" on the Lolo Trail.

The Expedition Endures

By Harry W. Fritz

The accomplishments of Lewis and Clark, nearly eclipsed by the end of the 1800s, have been returned to a place of honor during the past 50 years.

AS THE BICENTENNIAL OF THE EXPEDITION APPROACHES, the prestige of Lewis and Clark has never been higher, but their road to renown has been a twisted one. Not until the second half of the 20th century did the explorers achieve widespread celebrity.

Upon their return to the East in 1806, Lewis and Clark were heroes. But, as the 19th century wore on their reputation and awareness of their achievements faded from the national memory. Time and the rapid pace of progress eclipsed their accomplishments. Others reaped renown and fortune from the exploration and exploitation of the West. Although Lewis and Clark kept meticulous records and observations, most were not available to the general public. On some counts, such as Meriwether Lewis's claim to "have discovered the most practicable rout" across the continent, they were spectacularly wrong. Policies governing Indian trade and protection ended abruptly. Most of the place names they bestowed were forgotten and replaced. By century's end, Lewis and Clark were history.

Yet some Americans remembered. Montanans in 1871 renamed Edgerton County, honoring a Republican governor, with a new name – Lewis and Clark. The names of the Gallatin, Madison and Jefferson rivers, and many others survive. The President's instructions to Lewis served as a model for all future government-sponsored expeditions. William Clark's remarkable map of the Northwest, issued in 1814, remained in service for 40 years. When Isaac Stevens, a West Point engineer, prepared to lead a transcontinental railroad survey across the northern tier in 1853, he studied Clark's map.

Historian and editor William Goetzmann ends the Lewis and Clark era in 1820, but in reality it lasted for most of the 19th century. Lewis and Clark were the first Americans to explore, describe, and map the American West and others followed their example. In a larger sense, all government-sponsored exploration, even to the moon and Mars, is a legacy of Lewis and Clark. As Americans set out during the bicentennial to discover the West for themselves, they travel in the footsteps of Lewis and Clark.

In late-September 1806, Lewis and Clark started a triumphal return trip to the East. They stopped at Vincennes, Cahokia, Louisville; Lewis went on to Frankfort, Staunton, and Washington. Clark stayed home in Indiana for a while, then traveled

HORNED LIZARD/CHARLES WILLSON PEALE

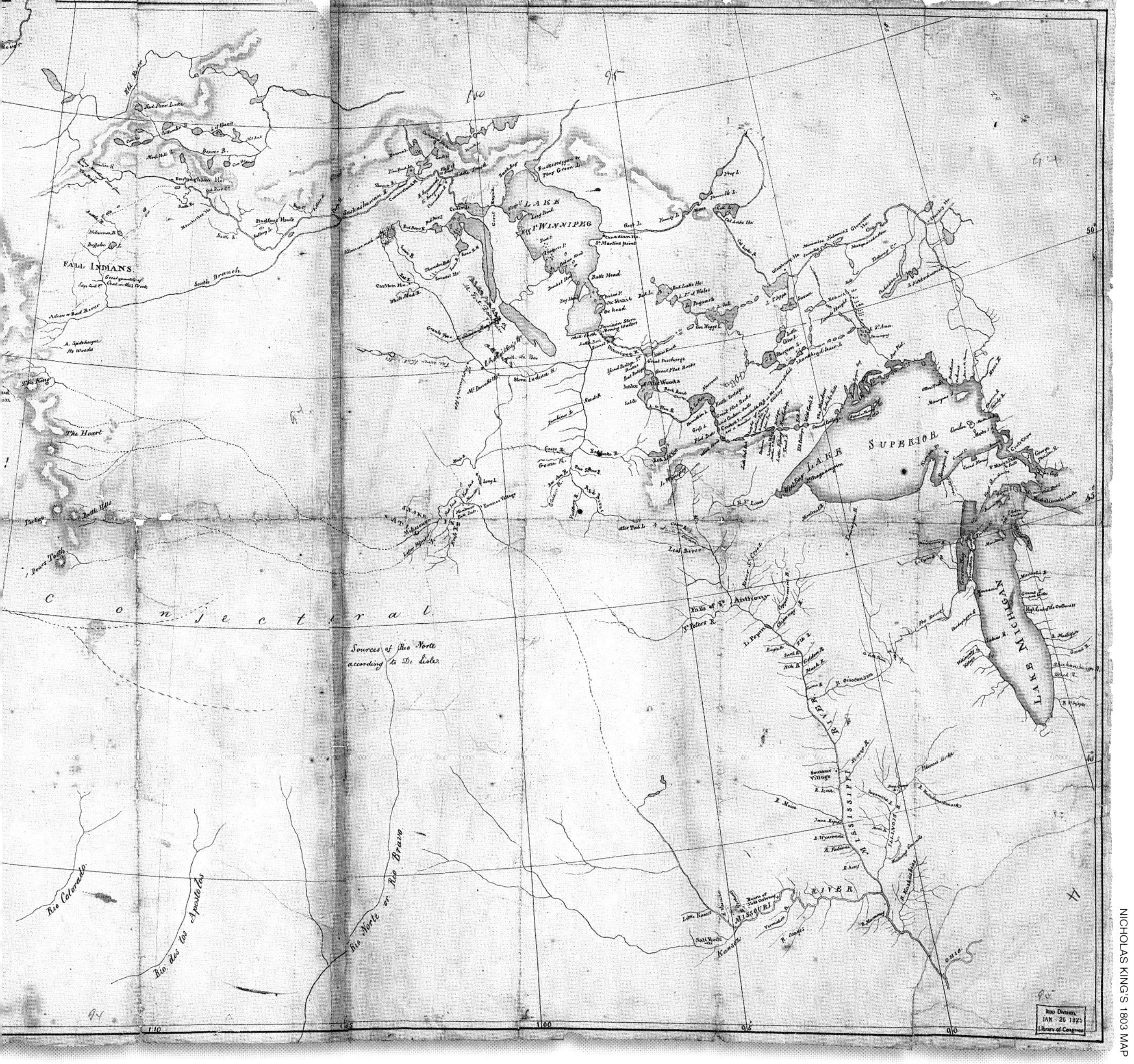

NICHOLAS KING'S 1803 MAP

to Fincastle, Virginia, where he became engaged. At each juncture, there were parades, banquets, orations, and poetry – most of it bad. The President welcomed Lewis on December 30, and staged a sumptuous banquet on January 14, 1807. Lewis went on to Philadelphia where he sat for his portrait with Charles Willson Peale (see page 3). All the while he made arrangements to bring out his priceless journals. Naturalist and author Paul Cutright summarizes: "He obtained a publisher, released a prospectus, engaged artists and naturalists to figure and describe his animal and plant specimens, persuaded still other draftsmen to make drawings of Indians and waterfalls, and induced a mathematician to correct navigational determinations." Nothing, not one word, resulted from these endeavors. Lewis suffered the worst case of writer's block in American history.

Lewis's papers from the Pacific were with him when he took his own life in Tennessee on October 11, 1809. Miraculously, they did not perish with him. James Neelly sent them to Washington. Clark picked them up there and took them to Philadelphia. Clark engaged Nicholas Biddle, a Federalist writer, as an editor.

Cartographer Nicholas King created this map from the best geographic sources in 1803 especially for the Lewis and Clark Expedition. While including Lake Michigan and the Mississippi and Missouri rivers in the Midwest and the Northwest's Pacific Coast line, little was known about America's interior. The explorers discovered the Rocky Mountains were more extensive than drawn here.

The illustration of the horned lizard (left) was made from a specimen collected by Lewis and Clark.

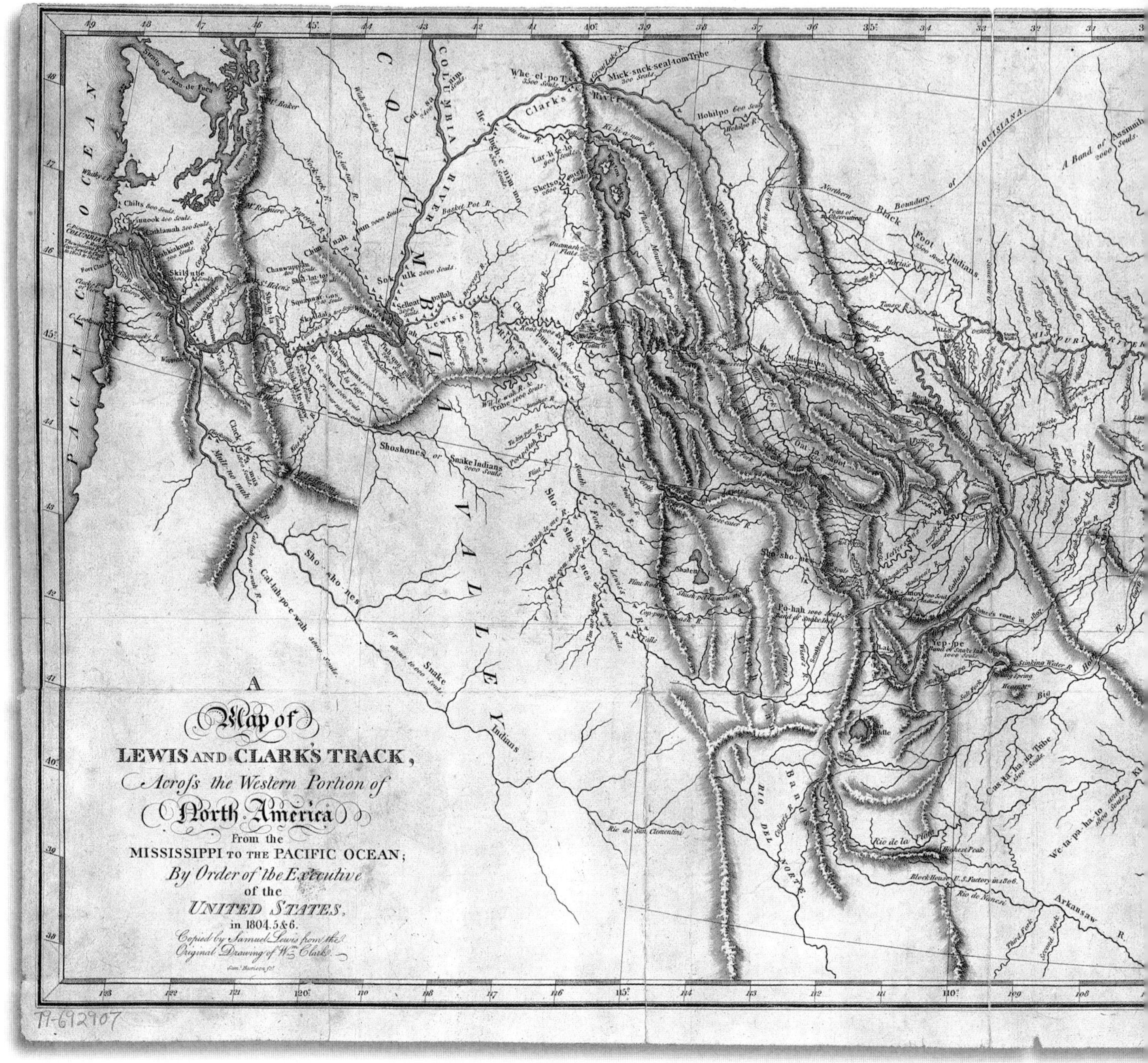

In 1814, Biddle issued a two-volume paraphrase as *The History of the Expedition.* The narrative omitted nearly all of the scientific data upon which the fame of Lewis and Clark now rests. Parts of it, dealing with sexual practices among Indians, appeared in Latin. Public interest, thanks to explorer Zebulon Pike and the War of 1812, had shifted. Only 2,000 copies were published, and they sold slowly. Clark never made a dime; he did not even acquire a copy for over a year. With little to sustain it, the reputation of Lewis and Clark faded.

When, nearly 80 years later, Elliott Coues (pronounced "cows") borrowed the original journals from the American Philosophical Society, he was astounded at the wealth of ethnological and biological information they contained. Coues's annotation of the Biddle edition (1893) first revealed to the public that the Expedition was something more than an extended hike. Finally, to mark the Expedition's centennial, Reuben Gold Thwaites published for the first time all of the original journals of Lewis and Clark.

In the meantime, more Lewis and Clark material came to light. Thwaites found some, in the possession of Clark's descendants in St. Louis. Biddle's grandsons turned over John Ordway's journal and Lewis's Ohio river journal in 1913.

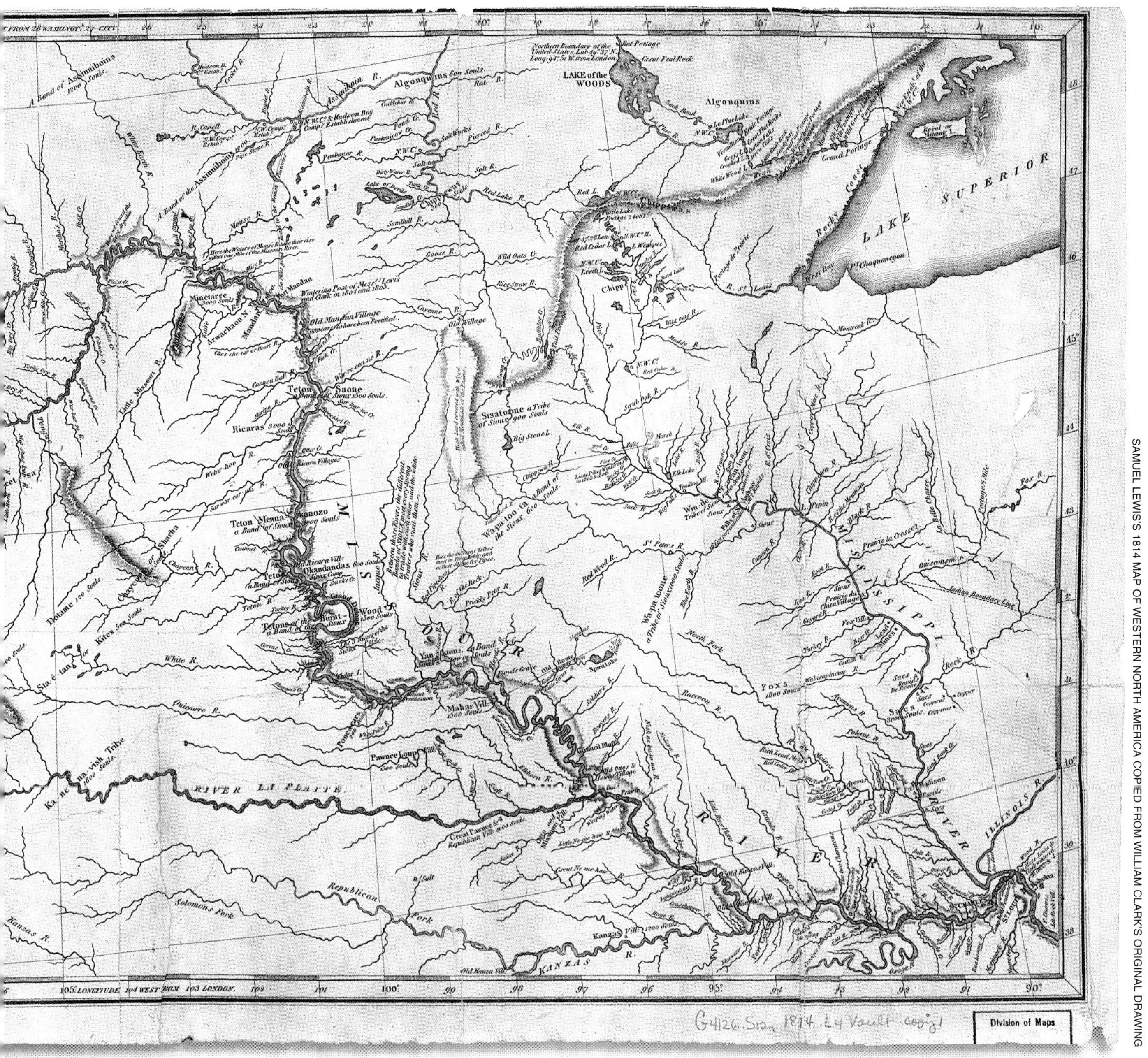

SAMUEL LEWIS'S 1814 MAP OF WESTERN NORTH AMERICA COPIED FROM WILLIAM CLARK'S ORIGINAL DRAWING

In contrast to King's map (pages 94-95), this map, copied in 1814 from an original drawing by William Clark, shows western North America from the Mississippi River to the Pacific Ocean with considerable detail. Clark's map, which included a wealth of details that he gathered from other travelers as they came through St. Louis, remained a primary source of information about the West for 40 years.

Clark's field notes appeared in an attic in Minneapolis in 1953. The first calls for a comprehensive, documented edition sounded.

The last 50 years have witnessed a resounding Lewis and Clark revival. The culmination of this enterprise is the magnificent 13-volume edition of *The Journals of the Lewis & Clark Expedition,* edited by Gary E. Moulton and published by the University of Nebraska Press (1983-2001).

Other Explorers Followed the Corps' Footsteps

Other Jeffersonian explorations occurred while Lewis and Clark were still in the field. William Dunbar and George Hunter went up the Ouachita River in 1804. Two years later, Thomas Freeman and Peter Custis went 635 miles up the Red River, only to be turned back by Spanish arms. Most peculiar was Zebulon Pike's unauthorized trip to Santa Fe. Pike was spying for General James Wilkinson, not exploring for Thomas Jefferson. Spaniards captured him on the Rio Grande and sent him home via Chihuahua. Pike's journals and maps upstaged Lewis and Clark and focused American attention on the Spanish Southwest.

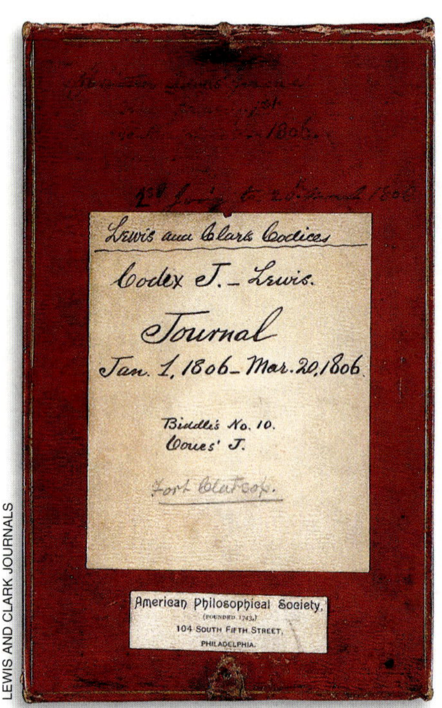

LEWIS AND CLARK JOURNALS

Lewis and Clark's small red morocco-bound notebooks, now carefully preserved in archives in Philadelphia and St. Louis, contain the daily records of their journey. It is from these volumes that historians and editors have told and interpreted the stories of the Expedition, again and again, over the past 200 years.

A German immigrant entrepreneur, John Jacob Astor, fulfilled the dreams of Lewis and Clark by building a fur trading post at the mouth of the Columbia River in 1811. The venture failed, thanks partly to the War of 1812, but not before Wilson Price Hunt led an overland expedition to Astoria on a route south of the Lewis and Clark trail. Returning east in 1813, another party followed the later Oregon Trail and discovered South Pass. Northwestern geography came into focus.

One more government expedition, led by Stephen H. Long in 1819-1820, mapped the Front Range of the Colorado Rockies. Thereafter, for a generation, exploration of the West became a private enterprise. Fur trappers and traders, including vaunted mountain men of legend and lore, pursued beaver and other animals into every promising drainage. When the government monopoly on Indian trade ended in the 1820s, other business opportunities appeared. Entrepreneurs also sought paths over the Rockies and through the Great Basin to California. Some of the most famous names in early western history sought profit as well as knowledge: William Ashley, Jedediah Smith, Joseph Walker, Jim Bridger. Their information appeared on maps and in guidebooks by the 1840s.

The government returned to its Jeffersonian duties under the auspices of the U.S. Corps of Topographical Engineers, established in 1838. Military engineers and mapmakers headed west to provide scientific foundations for amateur observations. Charles Wilkes sought suitable Pacific Coast ports. John C. Frémont, who understood both politics and public relations, crisscrossed the Far West and inspired the Bear Flag Revolt. Both the Mexican and Canadian borders were surveyed. Four well-equipped teams headed out to find suitable routes for a transcontinental railroad. After the Civil War, systematic surveys detailed most of the mountain West under what became, in 1879, the U.S. Geological Survey. The most noteworthy of these, headed by Ferdinand V. Hayden, covered both Nebraska and the new Yellowstone National Park.

Lewis and Clark would have approved. Their 1803 instructions from Jefferson were explicitly geographical and scientific. At every opportunity they recorded mathematical observations. Their legacy, Jefferson's legacy, did not expire with their Expedition. It lasted throughout the 19th century, and as a spirit of discovery, survives today.

What Happened to the Principals of the Expedition?

Jefferson's interest in the West declined precipitously after Lewis and Clark. Although he sent expeditions up the Ouachita and Red rivers, and approved of Pike' s erratic wanderings in the Colorado Rockies, his administration soon bogged down in domestic and diplomatic crises. In retirement, he devoted his energies to the founding of the University of Virginia. Editor and historian Donald Jackson provides the final reckoning: Although the Lewis and Clark era ended, the American West, "Jefferson' s remarkable monument," endured.

Lewis never wrote a line about his expedition for publication. His reward for his successful transcontinental journey was an appointment by Jefferson as Governor of Upper Louisiana, with headquarters in St. Louis. But Lewis was in over his head; he was a soldier, not a politician. His most insidious enemy, Territorial Secretary Frederick Bates, put it cruelly but accurately: "His habits are altogether military & he never can I think succeed in any other profession." Lewis foundered, incurred debts, and took to drink. In the fall of 1809, in a state of mental derangement on the Natchez Trace, he committed suicide.

Clark lived a long, productive, and procreative life after his Expedition. He married twice, and sired seven children. He held offices in Louisiana Territory as Brigadier General of Militia, Governor, and Superintendent of Indian Affairs. During the War of 1812 he led a military expedition up the Mississippi River against the British. He negotiated numerous treaties with midwestern Indians. Clark watched helplessly as the humanitarian and philanthropic policies he favored yielded to ruthless white expansion and private greed. He died peacefully

THE MISSOURI BELOW THE MOUTH OF THE PLATTE / KARL EODMER

on September 1, 1838, at the home of his eldest son, Meriwether Lewis Clark.

Sacagawea died in 1812, of "putrid fever." She may have visited St. Louis in 1810, with her husband Toussaint Charbonneau. Toussaint spent the rest of his life on the Missouri River, interpreting for a generation of travelers and traders. At age 80, he married a 14-year-old Assiniboin girl. He disappeared from history sometime around 1843. His son, Jean Baptiste, born at Fort Mandan in 1805, lived until 1866.

Clark's slave York obtained his freedom sometime after 1811, after earlier requesting it unsuccessfully. Clark subsidized him in the hauling business, but York went broke. He died of cholera in 1822.

John Colter is the most well-known member of the Expedition, aside from the principals, and the only one with a reputation earned after 1806. He returned to the Yellowstone Basin with Manuel Lisa' s Missouri Fur Company, and explored Wyoming and the Tetons.

Four members of the Expedition died violent deaths at the hands of Indians. The Blackfeet shot George Drouillard and John Potts near Three Forks in 1810; John Colter escaped. The Blackfeet may also have killed Peter Weiser in 1810, or thereafter. John Collins was killed by the Arikara in 1823. John Newman, court-martialed and expelled on the lower Missouri, was killed by the Yankton Sioux in 1838. One other member, George Shannon, escaped an Arikara attack in 1807 with only one leg.

The other Expedition members lived quietly and died the same. Most used their back pay and bonus money to buy farms. A few stayed in the Army, or re-enlisted. George Shannon became a lawyer. Sergeant Patrick Gass published his journal first, married at age 60, sired six children, and died in his 99th year, 1870, the Expedition's last survivor. But the Expedition itself endures.

Karl Bodmer's watercolor shows the blue effluent of the Platte River running along the right bank of the Missouri in May 1833. Clark passed this spot on July 21, 1804, and wrote, ". . . passed many Sand bars opposit or in the Mouth of the Great River Plate this river which is much more rapid than the Missourie ha[s] thrown out imence quantities of Sand . . ."

The Tribes: "We Have Survived"

By Gerard Baker

Lewis and Clark were not heroes to Indian people, but brought them only misery. The tribes may not celebrate the Expedition's bicentennial, but they can use the event as a chance to tell their side of the story.

I FIRST HEARD ABOUT LEWIS AND CLARK from the old timers and, of course, from my Mom and Dad. I can remember a lot of folks, relatives and friends of my folks, coming to visit us at our cattle ranch on the western side of the Fort Berthold Indian Reservation near our hometown of Mandaree, North Dakota. According to the elders, Lewis and Clark were no big deal and were certainly not heroes, in any sense of the word. In fact, they were just another group that came up the river to inform us that we had a "new Great White Father" and wanted to trade with us and other tribes.

It was not until I started to get interested in American history that I heard what role they played in the "discovery" of the new America. Of course, we all know that this America west of the Missouri River was not lost at all, but was the homeland of many organized tribes that already had well-established trade long before the coming of the Anglo. This trade was active in all Indian territories across this land from coast to coast.

The Indian tribes along the Missouri River saw their share of this trade as well, and also took part in various tribal networks between nomadic and agricultural tribes that lived here long before the famous American expedition known as the Corps of Discovery. What Lewis and Clark and their men saw is not only well documented in the journals, but has also been written about by many great past and contemporary authors. The American Indian side has also been written about in some great books, including one that is a favorite of mine and written by my

---

Gerard Baker of Omaha, Superintendent of the Lewis and Clark National Historic Trail with the National Park Service, is responsible for commemoration of the historic events that form the Trail's central theme. A full-blood member of the Mandan-Hidatsa Tribe of the Fort Berthold Indian Reservation, Baker has worked with 19 states and 58 tribes to bring to the forefront the story of American Indians, in their own words, during the bicentennial commemoration of the Voyage of Discovery.

IDOLS OF THE MANDAN INDIANS / KARL BODMER

In about 1833, Karl Bodmer painted these Mandan shrines, which the Mandans consulted before making significant decisions.

(ISCHOHA-KAKOSCHOCHATA0 DANCE OF THE MANDAN INDIANS / KARL BODMER

Karl Bodmer depicted this dance at Fort Clark on December 28, 1833. It is believed to show a ceremony of the Mandan Half-Shaved Society.

OMAHA BOY / KARL BODMER

With his face painted with vermillion and hair cut in a distinctive style, this Omaha boy was the subject of a Bodmer portrait in 1833.

friend James P. Ronda, *Lewis and Clark Among the Indians.* My spiritual brother, Dayton Duncan, who we gave the Hidatsa name of "he-who-goes-first," understands the American Indian side of things and writes about it in a way no other can. With all this said, I offer these impressions of what has happened to the tribes since the Lewis and Clark adventure, and I think more importantly, what is in the future. I offer these impressions, in part, from my perspective as the Superintendent of the Lewis and Clark National Historic Trail, located in the Midwest Regional Office of the National Park Service in Omaha.

Since the fall of 1999, I have been working to help commemorate the bicentennial of the Lewis and Clark Expedition years, which takes place from 2003 through 2006. One idea is to organize a mobile visitors center to explore this rediscovery and invite the American Indian people to tell their story in their own words. On this task, I have traveled the Lewis and Clark trail from coast to coast, and I have had the privilege of visiting many tribes whose ancestors were in contact with the Corps of Discovery.

Indians Retain Pride in Way of Life

If we look at the overall experience since then, and we think about those tribes and what has happened to them, it is not a pretty story. But, if we look at the Indian people themselves, I believe, we still see the pride, and some of the way of life that the crew saw in the early-1800s, even if some of this way of life may now survive only in a philosophical sense.

The story of the tribes in the past 200 years has been one of defeat, relocation and putting their culture behind them in the name of survival, according to many of the Indian people I have had the opportunity to visit. In the name of "western expansion" and "manifest destiny" we have seen many of the tribes of Nebraska moved to Indian Territory, which is now the state of Oklahoma. Those tribes include the Oto, Missouria, Ponca and Pawnee, which were some of the same groups that Lewis and Clark hoped to meet along the Missouri River. It was not until the council bluff camp, near present-day Fort Calhoun, Nebraska, in August of 1804 that they met Indian people, some of the Otos and Missourias, but not the two main chiefs, Little Thief and Big Horse. It is interesting to note that many tribal folks I have visited said that Lewis and Clark are the ones who identified and actually made many of the people in the different groups "chiefs." Some elders told me that they never had first, second or third chiefs until the Lewis and Clark Expedition. The feeling of the tribal groups is that the tribes have been and often still are looked upon as second-class citizens in this country. When one looks at the reservation system, early government schools and the complete change of life, it's little wonder that they have those feelings.

Three Elements Changed Indian Life

This has all happened in the 200 years since Lewis and Clark. It is felt by many Indian people the three factors with greatest effects on Indian people and our country were the fur traders, organized Christianity and the U.S. Government.

Fur traders, the elders say, changed the way of life by the introduction of iron implements among other items. Before this introduction, the Indian people used all natural items, either taken from the animals they killed or from the plants they secured. The belief was that these items were alive and were therefore respected and treated like they were alive because they had a spirit. Iron implements, on the other hand, have been looked upon as not being alive, and the concept of the spirit started to diminish.

When Christianity came into Indian country, it caused confusion and doubt, according to the elders. The early missionaries stated that our religion was one of worshipping false idols and not a "true God." They removed medicine bundles, most of the time forcibly, and each group "fought for the souls of the Indian." They did not realize that the medicines that we Indians obtained were given to us by the Creator, and if they had taken the time to understand, they would have seen that the Indian religion is based on respect for ourselves and for the earth.

The last major factor, according to many elders I have spoken to, was the U.S. Government. This involved Indian removal, early education and the notion that, in order to survive, the Indian people had to assimilate into the Anglo society. One of the basic ways to do this, of course, is to take away traditional language from Indian children. This was done in many instances.

I have heard these same thoughts all along the Lewis and Clark trail, but I have also heard loud and clear that "we have survived this," and if there is anything to celebrate with the bicentennial of the Lewis and Clark Expedition, it is the fact that the American Indian people are still here and are working on that survival. Many of the Indian people now say they recognize the need to live and learn in two worlds, first and foremost the need to relearn, or in a lot of cases, keep learning our traditions and languages. They were not lost, but were simply put to the side in the name of survival. I have heard in Indian country that we still have our traditions, that we need to keep teaching them, that we need to help all peoples understand who we are, and that we do have a future.

Indian people see the Lewis and Clark years, not as a celebration, but as a commemoration and a positive opportunity to tell the Indian side of the story. We must listen to all sides and understand that, in all these years, there are some very negative but real stories, but there are also many beautiful stories of Indian people.

There is also much hope for the future, and that future is in the next generation and those not yet born. The elders along the trail say we are all proud of who we are, that we must to show that pride in what we do, that we must learn from the past to have a successful future, and that we must never, never lose our identity as American Indians.

DACOTA WOMAN / KARL BODMER

Karl Bodmer painted this portrait at Fort Pierre, South Dakota, on June 1, 1833. The "Dacota woman" is wearing a dress of deer or elk hide trimmed in blue and white beads, with a fringe of twisted metal cones at the hem, which made a tinkling sound when she walked. Over the dress she is wrapped in a summer robe of buffalo hide with the hair removed. The box-and-border geometric pattern was popular among Plains tribes.

Traveling with Lewis and Clark

By Eric Fowler

Picturesque, historical and entertaining sites line the Missouri River along the trail blazed by Lewis and Clark in 1804. Today the trek is easier, but the journey is still a worthy adventure.

IN 1804, LEWIS AND CLARK and a party of 44 men left Camp River Dubois in Illinois and 173 days later, after covering 1,641 miles on the Missouri River, established their winter camp near Mandan and Hidatsa villages in North Dakota. Today, the quickest overland route between the same points – about 1,080 miles – would take a day or two to drive.

But, many of the millions of people who are expected to retrace parts of America's great adventure story during the next few years will do so for the journey, not to make a speedy trip to a destination.

To retrace part of the trail that the explorers covered in 1804, travel to any point on the Missouri River below Washburn, North Dakota, and follow the river. Along the way, you will find museums, visitor centers and a growing number of roadside markers that explain the Corps of Discovery's journey. Whether your interest is understanding the trail's natural history, geography, American Indians or coming to grips with the pivotal role the Expedition played in American history, there are plenty of opportunities to learn and to have fun.

Modern-day explorers following the trail will find more than Lewis and Clark. The travelers' guide on the following pages highlights some of the historical and scenic sites and attractions along the Missouri River corridor from St. Louis to Washburn, North Dakota.

Whenever you take the journey, whatever your interests, wherever you start, don't be in a hurry. Let the spectacular scenery along the river – the same beauty that entranced Lewis and Clark – soak in. Take a hike. Catch some fish. Find a back road that follows the river through farm or ranch country. Stop at a small-town diner and talk with people. If you don't make it as far as you had planned, don't worry. The trail isn't going anywhere and, unlike the men in the Corps of Discovery, you don't have to get there before winter sets in.

ERIC FOWLER

Cabins at Niobrara State Park overlook an unchannelized stretch of the Missouri River lined with backwaters and islands.

Washburn
Bismarck
NORTH DAKOTA
Missouri River
Mobridge
SOUTH DAKOTA
Pierre
Bad River
Chamberlain
Vermillion
Yankton
Niobrara
Floyd River
Niobrara River
NEBRASKA
Platte River
KANSAS
45
44
43
42
41
40
39
38
37
36
35
34
33
32
31
30
1 inch = about 58 miles

Retracing the 1804 Trail Today

The numbered red dots on this map mark sites of interest along the Missouri River corridor, beginning in the St. Louis area and moving upstream to Washburn, North Dakota. The numbers correspond to the photographs and descriptions about the sites on the following pages. Where there are several attractions in the same small area – Omaha, Nebraska, for example – the attractions share the same number on the map. A ■ symbol indicates there is a photo from this site.

For more information, contact state tourism offices and ask about sites along the Lewis and Clark trail.

Missouri Division of Tourism
(800) 810-5500
www.visitmo.com

Kansas Travel and Tourism
(800) 2KANSAS (252-6727)
www.travelks.com

Nebraska Division of Travel and Tourism
(877) NEBRASKA (632-7275)
www.visitnebraska.org

Iowa Division of Tourism
(888) 472-6035
www.traveliowa.com

South Dakota Department of Tourism
(800) S-DAKOTA (732-5682)
www.travelsd.com

North Dakota Tourism Division
(800) HELLO ND (435-5663)
www.ndtourism.com

JEFFERSON NATIONAL EXPANSION MEMORIAL

The Old Courthouse (foreground) and the Gateway Arch are part of the Jefferson National Expansion Memorial on the banks of the Mississippi River in St. Louis.

MISSOURI DEPARTMENT OF NATURAL RESOURCES

The Katy Trail, a rails-to-trails project, stretches nearly the entire width of Missouri, following the Missouri River for 154 miles from St. Charles to Boonville.

Missouri and Illinois

1 Lewis and Clark State Historic Site and Visitor Center

South of Hartford, Illinois. Located on the east bank of the Mississippi River across from its confluence with the Missouri River, this park is near the spot where the Lewis and Clark Expedition began. Opening in August 2002, this new visitor center is devoted entirely to the Expedition, especially the story of Corps' first winter encampment at nearby Camp River Dubois. Displays include state-of-the-art electronic and hands-on exhibits, a theater, and a full-sized keelboat replica. A memorial to the journey stands on the banks of the Mississippi. Illinois Historic Preservation Agency. Free. (618) 251-5393. www.campdubois.com

2 Jefferson National Expansion Memorial ■

St. Louis, Missouri. The Gateway Arch, rising 630-feet above the banks of the Mississippi River, stands as a monument to westward expansion where it all began. Below the arch, the Museum of Westward Expansion documents the movement west. A short walk away is the Old Courthouse, where in 1828 slave Dred Scott asked for his freedom and which now features displays that trace the history of the St. Louis riverfront. The museum and courthouse are free. A fee is charged for rides to the top of the arch and for rides on a Mississippi riverboat. National Park Service (NPS). (314) 655-1700. www.nps.gov/jeff

2 Missouri History Museum

St. Louis, Missouri. William Clark's journal and other Expedition artifacts are part of the museum's extensive Lewis and Clark collection. In 2004, the museum, located in Forest Park, will present Lewis & Clark: The National Bicentennial Exhibition, a collection of artifacts from the journey. (See story on opposite page about the Bicentennial Exhibition). Free. (314) 746-4599. www.mohistory.org/Exhibits4.html

2 William Clark Gravesite

St. Louis, Missouri. Located in Bellefontaine Cemetery, a bust of the explorer and a granite obelisk face the confluence of the Mississippi and Missouri rivers. The cemetery is open daily. Maps are available to guide visitors to the Clark gravesite. Free.

2 Columbia Bottoms Conservation Area

Near St. Louis, south of the confluence of the Missouri and Mississippi rivers in St. Louis County. This largely unimproved area, which includes 6½ miles of riverfront, is tentatively set to reopen in 2003 following access improvements, including a new road, hiking and biking trail, and river access at the confluence. Missouri Department of Conservation (MDC). Free. (636) 441-4554. www.conservation.state.mo.us/areas/areas/bottom

2 State Park at the Confluence

Near St. Louis, north of the confluence of the Mississippi and Missouri rivers in St. Charles County. Yet to be officially named and tentatively scheduled to open in 2004, this new park will include a trail to the confluence as well as interpretive information about the Lewis and Clark Expedition, which began across the river. Missouri Department of Natural Resources (MDNR). Free. (800) 334-6946. www.mostateparks.com

3 Lewis and Clark Boathouse and Nature Center

St. Charles, Missouri. Hand-painted dioramas, a campsite and nature trail are found at the center, which is located in St. Charles' historical district, a popular stop for history buffs and travelers in this town where the Expedition camped for a few days while Lewis completed preparations for the journey in St. Louis. Admission charged. (636) 947-3199. www.lewisandclarkcenter.org

3 Katy Trail State Park ■

St. Charles to Clinton, Missouri. The longest completed rails-to-trails project in the nation, the 225-mile-long Katy Trail stretches across most of the state. The trail follows the Missouri River for 154 miles from St. Charles to Boonville and is designated as a segment of the Lewis and Clark National Historic Trail. The landscape is varied, scenery spectacular and wildlife abundant along the trail. Trailheads have been developed in most communities, many of which offer services catering to hikers and bikers. Horses are permitted between Sedalia and Calhoun. MDNR. Free. (800) 334-6946. www.mostateparks.com/katytrail.htm

4 Wine Country

Augusta, Washington and Hermann. Award-winning wines can be sampled at wineries in these communities located in the scenic Missouri River Valley. www.missouriwine.org

5 Clark's Hill/Norton State Historic Site

Six miles east of Jefferson City, Missouri. While camped at the confluence of the Osage and Missouri rivers on June 1, 1804, Clark climbed what historians believe to be this hill and observed what he described in his journal as the "delightful prospect" of both rivers. Acquired in 2002, tentative plans call for constructing a trail to the hilltop and interpretive displays by 2004. MDNR. (800) 334-6946. www.mostateparks.com

5 Missouri State Museum

Jefferson City, Missouri. Located in the Missouri State Capitol, the museum features historical and contemporary displays. Visitors will also find statues of Lewis, Clark and Sacagawea in the capitol. Outside, a prominent statue of Thomas Jefferson greets visitors on one side of the building while on the other side, on a terrace overlooking the Missouri River, a bronze relief depicts the signing of the Louisiana Purchase. MDNR. Free. (573) 751-2854. www.mostateparks.com/jeffersonland/capitolinfo.htm

5 Jefferson Landing State Historic Site

Jefferson City, Missouri. This rare, surviving Missouri River landing, a block away from the state capitol, has exhibits of life in the 1800s and includes some original buildings that served the steamboat trade as early as 1839. MDNR. Free. (573) 751-2854. www.mostateparks.com/jeffersonland.htm

5 Runge Conservation Nature Center

Jefferson City, Missouri. Visitors can learn about Missouri's varied landscape and habitats inside the center and on nature trails. MDC. Free. (573) 526-5544. www.conservation.state.mo.us/areas/cnc/runge

6 Mark Twain National Forest, Cedar Creek Ranger District

North of Jefferson City, Missouri. One of the largest areas of public land north of the Missouri River, the area includes forests and restored tallgrass prairie and offers 36 miles of hiking trails, picnicking, camping and fishing.

MISSOURI HISTORICAL SOCIETY, ST. LOUIS, ALLIED PHOTOCOLOR

Clark's elkskin journal will be among the artifacts featured in Lewis & Clark: The National Bicentennial Exhibition.

The National Bicentennial Exhibition

The largest collection of Lewis and Clark artifacts assembled since the Expedition ended in 1806 will begin a three-year tour of the country at the Missouri History Museum in St. Louis in January 2004.

Lewis & Clark: The National Bicentennial Exhibition will include some of the specimens collected by the explorers, maps, art, manuscripts, equipment and Captain William Clark's personal elkskin journal.

Some of the 40 exhibition lenders include: National Museum of American History, Smithsonian Institution; Peabody Museum, Harvard University; Monticello; Library of Congress; American Philosophical Society; and the National Archives.

Presented by the Missouri Historical Society, the exhibit is supported by the National Park Service and The Missouri Lewis & Clark Bicentennial Commission.

The Exhibition Schedule

- Missouri History Museum, St. Louis, January 14, 2004-September 6, 2004.
- Academy of Natural Sciences of Philadelphia, November 2004-March 2005.
- Denver Museum of Nature and Science, Denver, May 2005-September 2005.
- Oregon Historical Society, Portland, November 2005-March 2006.
- National Museum of Natural History, Smithsonian Institution, Washington, D.C., May 2006-September 2006.

MISSOURI DEPARTMENT OF NATURAL RESOURCES

The rock bridge is one of many unique geologic formations at Rock Bridge State Park near Columbia, Missouri.

USDA Forest Service. Suggested donation. (573) 592-1400. www.fs.fed.us/r9/marktwain/ranger-districts/cedarcreek/cedar_creek_index.htm

7 Rock Bridge Memorial State Park ■

Two miles south of Columbia, Missouri. Sinkholes, caves and underground streams are part of the unique karst topography of the park. The park offers picnicking and 22 miles of hiking, biking and horse trails. MDNR. Free. (573) 449-7402. www.mostateparks.com/rockbridge.htm

7 Thomas Jefferson's Original Grave Marker

Columbia, Missouri. A six-foot obelisk that once sat at Monticello next to the grave of Jefferson, the president who launched the Corps of Discovery, now rests at the University of Missouri-Columbia, the first public university established in the Louisiana Purchase. The marker is located in the Thomas Jefferson Garden, which also includes a bronze sculpture of the president. Free. (800) 856-2181 or (573) 882-6333.

7 University of Missouri-Columbia Anthropology Museum

Columbia, Missouri. The only anthropology museum in Missouri and one of the few in the Midwest, the museum has the largest holding of prehistoric Missouri artifacts in the world. It also holds thousands of ethnographic objects from many cultures around the world, including a collection of Native American artifacts. Free. (573) 882-3573. http://coas.missouri.edu/AnthroMuseum

8 Les Bourgeois Vineyards

Rocheport, Missouri. Winery offers a restaurant and wine garden with a bluff-top view of the Missouri River. (573) 698-2133. www.missouriwine.com

9 Lyceum Theatre

Arrow Rock, Missouri. Broadway-style shows are held each summer in this 408-seat church-turned-theater. Admission charged. (660) 837-3311. www.lyceumtheatre.org

9 Arrow Rock State Historic Site

Arrow Rock, Missouri. Once a thriving river community, this entire town is now a National Historic Landmark. The historical site includes a visitor center, hiking trails and campground. MDNR. Free. (660) 837-3330. www.mostateparks.com/arrowrock.htm

9 Boone's Lick State Historic Site

Twelve miles northwest of Boonville, Missouri. The largest of many saltwater springs identified by Lewis and Clark as they passed through the region in 1804 was later named Boone's Lick. In 1805, two sons of Daniel Boone and others formed a partnership to use water from the spring to produce salt needed in pioneer times to preserve meat and tan hides. A short trail winds its way to the spring site where wood remnants of the salt works and an iron kettle are still visible. MDNR. (660) 837-3330. www.mostateparks.com/booneslick.htm

10 Van Meter State Park

Twelve miles northwest of Marshall, Missouri. The park features the "old fort," a six-acre, Missouria Indian earthwork construction of unknown purpose. The park also features Indian burial mounds that predate the Missouria, a visitor center, hiking trails, campground, picnic area, and a fishing lake. MDNR. Free. (660) 886-7537 www.mostateparks.com/vanmeter.htm

11 The Battle of Lexington State Historic Site

Lexington, Missouri. A house at the site where the park is now located was the prize for three days of bloody Civil War fighting between the Union Army

TOM WHITE

Reconstructed Fort Osage, originally built in 1808, overlooks the Missouri River near Sibley, Missouri. The Expedition camped on the opposite side of the river in 1804.

and Missouri State Guard. The restored building still carries scars from shells, and graves of unknown Union soldiers and remnants of trenches dot the 100-acre battlefield. A visitor center includes exhibits from the events of 1861. MDNR. Admission charged to tour the house. Entrance to grounds is free. (660) 259-4654. www.mostateparks.com/lexington/lexington.htm

⓬ Fort Osage National Historic Landmark ■
Sibley, Missouri. The second military outpost in the Louisiana Purchase, Fort Osage was built under the direction of William Clark in 1808 on a high spot overlooking the Missouri River that he had identified in 1804 as a potential fort site. Today's fort was reconstructed from original plans. Open weekends year-round, and from Wednesday through Sunday, April 15 to November 15. Jackson County Parks and Recreation. Admission charged. (816) 795-8200 ext. 1-260. www.historicfortosage.com

⓭ National Frontier Trails Center
Independence, Missouri. The Center tells the story of the exploration, acquisition and settlement of the American West through a film and interpretive exhibits of the Santa Fe, Oregon and California trails, all of which went though Independence. A Trail Blazers exhibit features Lewis and Clark. City of Independence. Admission charged. (816) 325-7575. www.frontiertrailscenter.com

⓭ Clark's Point ■
Kansas City, Missouri. Located in Case Park at Eighth and Jefferson streets, this spot overlooks the confluence of the Missouri and Kansas rivers and features a bronze statue of Lewis, Clark, Sacagawea, York and Lewis's dog, Seaman.

⓭ Steamboat Arabia Museum
Kansas City, Missouri. The museum tells the story of how the *Arabia* sank in the Missouri River in 1856 and was recovered 132 years later. The cargo is on display. Admission charged. (816) 471-1856. www.1856.com

A statue depicting Sacagawea, Clark, Lewis, York and Lewis's dog, Seaman (back of statue) stands on Clark's Point in Kansas City, Missouri.

Missouri and Kansas

⓭ Kaw Point
Kansas City, Kansas. Improvements, including a floodwall mural and historical markers are planned and may be complete by early-2004 at Kaw Point, located at the mouth of the Kansas River, where Lewis and Clark camped for several days. Kansas City, Kansas/Wyandotte County Convention & Visitors Bureau. Free. (913) 321-5800.

⓭ Old Shawnee Town
Shawnee, Kansas. This authentically reproduced rural frontier town includes buildings and historical artifacts from the 1800s and early-1900s. Open February through mid-December. Shawnee Parks and Recreation. Admission charged. (913) 248-2360. www.cityofshawnee.org/parks/OldShawneeTown/oldshawneetown.htm

⓭ Shawnee Indian Mission State Historic Site
Fairway, Kansas. A National Historic Landmark, the mission served as an early territorial capital, a supply point

ERIC FOWLER

Visitors to the Frontier Army Museum at Fort Leavenworth, Kansas, find an 1836 six-pounder cannon and other military artifacts at the oldest Army installation in continuous service west of the Mississippi River.

on the Santa Fe and Oregon Trails, and a camp for Union soldiers during the Civil War. It was a school attended by Shawnee, Delaware and other Indian nations from 1839 to 1862. Kansas State Historical Society. Donation suggested. (913) 262-0867. www.kshs.org/places/shawnmis.htm

13 Wyandotte County Historical Society Museum

Bonner Springs, Kansas. Museum includes an exhibit about the Lewis and Clark Expedition. Free. (913) 721-1078. www.kumc.edu/wcedc/museum/wcmuseum.html

MISSOURI DEPARTMENT OF NATURAL RESOURCES

Lewis and Clark Lake, which William Clark called Gosling Lake, is an oxbow in Lewis and Clark State Park near Rushville, Missouri. The lake draws anglers, boaters and others who are looking for a relaxing spot.

13 National Agricultural Center and Hall of Fame

Bonner Springs, Kansas. Federally chartered and privately funded, the center features the National Farmer's Memorial, National Agriculture Hall of Fame, Museum of Farming, Gallery of Rural Art and a turn-of-the-century rural village. Admission charged. (913) 721-1075. www.aghalloffame.com

14 Leavenworth Landing Park

Leavenworth, Kansas. This Missouri River park includes a walking trail and artwork that focuses on Leavenworth's role as the "Gateway to the West." Leavenworth Convention & Visitors Bureau. Free. (913) 682-4113. www.lvarea.com/cvb/attracts.htm

14 Frontier Army Museum ■

Fort Leavenworth, Kansas. The museum features artifacts of Frontier Army soldiers who served west of the Mississippi River between 1804 and 1917. It includes an exhibit on the Lewis and Clark Expedition, which also is highlighted in a series of wayside exhibits at the fort, the oldest Army installation in continuous service west of the Mississippi River. The fort also features a monument to the black soldiers on the frontier, who were known as Buffalo Soldiers. Donation suggested. (913) 684-3191. http://leav-www.army.mil/museum

15 Weston Bend State Park ■
Weston, Missouri. Located in forested hills along the Missouri River, this park includes an interpretive exhibit about the tobacco industry that followed settlement in the area and continues today. It offers camping, picnicking, a hiking and biking trail and a scenic river overlook. MDNR. Free. (816) 640-5443. www.mostateparks.com/westonbend.htm

16 Lewis and Clark State Park ■
South of Rushville, Missouri. The park is located on the banks of Lewis and Clark Lake, an oxbow described and named by Clark in his journals as Gosling Lake for all the geese and goslings he saw there in 1804. It features interpretive displays on the Expedition as well as camping, picnicking, fishing, swimming and boating. MDNR. Free. (816) 579-5564. www.mostateparks.com/lewisandclark.htm

16 Atchison County Historical Society Museum
Atchison, Kansas. Includes Lewis and Clark displays. Suggested donation. (913) 367-6238. www.atchison.kansas.net/tourism/histsoct.htm

17 St. Joseph Museum
St. Joseph, Missouri. The museum contains a collection of Missouri wildlife and exhibits featuring American Indians, Lewis and Clark, the Civil War, the Pony Express and Jesse James. Admission charged. (816) 232-8471. www.stjosephmuseum.org

17 Pony Express Museum
St. Joseph, Missouri. Museum depicts the famous overland mail service, which began in St. Joseph in 1860. Admission charged. (816) 279-5059 or (800) 530-5930. www.ponyexpress.org

MISSOURI DEPARTMENT OF NATURAL RESOURCES

A viewing deck at Weston Bend State Park near Weston, Missouri, provides visitors a high vantage point overlooking the Missouri River.

17 National Military Heritage Museum
St. Joseph, Missouri. The museum features exhibits and history of all five branches of the U.S. Military – Army, Navy, Marines, Air Force, and Coast Guard. Admission charged. (816) 233-4321. www.nationalmilitaryheritagemuseum.org/

ERIC FOWLER

Visitors to Indian Cave State Park near Shubert, Nebraska, follow a walkway along the front of the cave, the site of ancient petroglyphs.

18 Native American Heritage Museum State Historic Site

Three miles east of Highland, Kansas. Museum tells the story of the Great Lakes Indian tribes forced to emigrate to Kansas following Lewis and Clark's Expedition. The museum building was built in 1848 as a Presbyterian mission for the Sac and Fox Indians, whose reservation is a few miles to the north. Kansas State Historical Society. Suggested donation. (785) 442-3304. www.kshs.org/places/highland.htm

19 Squaw Creek National Wildlife Refuge

Three miles southwest of Mound City, Missouri. A wintering area for large numbers of bald eagles and a stopping point for snow geese during their fall migration south, the refuge, which includes Missouri River floodplain marsh and loess hills prairie, is home to 301 bird species, 33 different mammals and 35 amphibian and reptile species. A self-guided auto tour, hiking trails and picnicking are available. U.S. Fish and Wildlife Service (USFWS). Free. (660) 442-3187. http://midwest.fws.gov/SquawCreek

19 Big Lake State Park

Eleven miles southwest of Mound City, Missouri. Missouri's largest oxbow lake is a popular boating and fishing spot. A marsh on one end of the oxbow is a major attraction for migratory and resident birds and an example of the habitat created by the wandering Missouri River. The park offers picnicking, swimming, camping, a restaurant and cabins and other lodging. MDNR. Free. (660) 442-3770. www.mostateparks.com/biglake.htm

Nebraska and Iowa

20 Indian Cave State Park ■

Two miles north and five miles east of Shubert, Nebraska. Ancient petroglyphs are found on the walls of the huge sandstone cavity that gives this park its name. The park offers camping, horseback riding and 20 miles of trails in wooded bluffs along the Missouri River. Living-history presentations on summer weekends include broom-making and blacksmithing, and visitors will also find a restored one-room brick schoolhouse built in 1908 in the old town of St. Deroin. Nebraska Game and Parks Commission (NGPC). Nebraska park entry permit required. (402) 883-2575. http://www.ngpc.state.ne.us/parks/showpark.ihtml?area_No=91

21 Brownville State Recreation Area

Brownville, Nebraska. Located on the banks of the Missouri River in historical Brownville, the area offers boating access to the Missouri, fishing, camping and picnicking. NGPC. Nebraska park entry permit required. (402) 883-2575. http://www.ngpc.state.ne.us/parks/showpark.ihtml?area_No=36

21 Museum of Missouri River History

Brownville, Nebraska. Located in the *Captain Meriwether Lewis*, a dry-docked dredge boat that helped channelize the Missouri River, the museum's exhibits detail development of the Missouri River Valley. Open afternoons on weekends from April through October and on weekdays from Memorial Day weekend through Labor Day. Admission charged. (402) 825-3341.

21 Spirit of Brownville ■

Brownville, Nebraska. Riverboat offers history and dinner cruises to the public on the Missouri River weekends in June, July and August, or by charter April through October. Fee charged. (402) 825-6441. www.spiritofbrownville.com

21 Steamboat Trace Hiking and Biking Trail

Brownville to near Nebraska City, Nebraska. This 21-mile, rails-to-trails project skirts the Missouri River Valley, with trailheads in Brownville, Peru and six miles south of Nebraska City. Open to hiking and biking only. Voluntary donations accepted. Nemaha Natural Resources District. (402) 335-3325. www.nemahanrd.org/

22 Wabash Trace Nature Trail

Blanchard (southern border) to Council Bluffs, Iowa. This 63-mile hiking and biking trail follows the loess hills from Iowa's southern border near Blanchard to Council Bluffs, with trailheads in Coin, Shenandoah, Imogene, Malvern, Silver City and Mineola. Horses are permitted between Mineola and Council Bluffs, where the trail connects with Lake Manawa State Park and the Western Historic Trails Center. Southwest Iowa Nature Trails Inc. Trail user pass required. (712) 246-4444. http://wabashtrace.heartland.net

23 Loess Hills National Scenic Byway

Hamburg to Akron, Iowa. More than 220 miles of roads, stretching from Iowa's southern border to north of Sioux City with 16 excursion loops in between, make up this scenic drive through Iowa's loess hills. This unique landform was created near the end of the last Ice Age by fine windblown soil and makes up the eastern edge of the Missouri River Valley. Golden Hills RC & D. Free. (712) 482-3029. www.goldenhillsrcd.org/byway

23 Waubonsie State Park ■

Four miles south and two west of Sidney, Iowa. This scenic park in the Loess Hills offers camping, picnicking, seven miles of foot trails and eight miles of equestrian trails. It's one of the best places in the region to see the changing fall colors. Iowa Department of Natural Resources (IDNR). Free. (712) 382-2786. www.state.ia.us/dnr/organiza/ppd/waubonsi.htm

24 Lewis and Clark Interpretive Trail and Visitor's Center

Nebraska City, Nebraska. Scheduled to open in 2003, the center will focus on the flora and fauna discovered by the Expedition – a theme not covered by any other center. The center will also feature a full-scale replica keelboat and serve as a trailhead for the Steamboat Trace Trail. Admission charged. Contact Nebraska City Chamber of Commerce. (402) 873-6654.

24 Arbor Lodge State Historical Park and Arboretum

Nebraska City, Nebraska. Arbor Lodge, the elegant 52-room neo-colonial style mansion built by J. Sterling Morton, founder of Arbor Day, is the centerpiece of this park. The grounds are open year-round and the mansion is open April through October. NGPC. Nebraska park entry permit required. Admission charged to tour mansion. (402) 873-7222. www.ngpc.state.ne.us/parks/showpark.ihtml?area_No=4

ERIC FOWLER

Jim and Deanna Matthews of Papillion, Nebraska, wave from the railing of the *Spirit of Brownville* riverboat as it passes Indian Cave State Park near Schubert, Nebraska. The boat offers rides on the Missouri River from Brownville.

ERIC FOWLER

Frank Tomkinson and Jill Mace of Omaha follow a ridgetop trail at Waubonsie State Park in the loess hills near Hamburg, Iowa.

Lewis & Clark Living History

By Ken Bouc

KEN BOUC

Bob Soukup of Discovery Corps, Inc. fires the swivel gun.

Attractions along Lewis and Clark's route are made more enjoyable and educational by a dedicated cadre of living historians dressed and equipped as members of the Expedition, trained in the skills they used on their epic journey, and fluent in the Lewis and Clark lore they pass on to the public. Most are history buffs, organized into groups ranging from a half-dozen members to well over 100, with one thing in common – a drive to research and understand some aspect of the Lewis and Clark story, and an eagerness to adopt the persona of a Lewis and Clark character and bring to life what they have learned.

KEN BOUC

The camp of **The Discovery Expedition of St. Charles, Missouri, Inc.** gives two young visitors a rich and entertaining taste of living history in keeping with the group's mission. In its replica keelboat and pirogues, The Discovery Expedition will retrace the Corps of Discovery's 1804 trek to winter quarters at Fort Mandan in 2004. The St. Charles group has 175 trained crew members hailing from points as distant as Pennsylvania, California, Mississippi and Montana. The group will also host a national signature event May 15-23, 2004. Contact Discovery Expedition of St. Charles through the Lewis and Clark Boathouse and Nature Center, 1050 Riverside Drive, St. Charles, by phone (636) 947-3199; or web site, www.lewisandclark.net

RON UKRAINETZ

Lewis and Clark Honor Guard of Great Falls, Montana recreates the Corps of Discovery's grueling portage around the Great Falls of the Missouri River in June and July, 1805. The portage is the group's primary focus, but it also participates in events throughout Montana. All of the Honor Guard's 67 active members are familiar with or fluent in native sign language, and several speak French. Each member researches and portrays at least two members of the Expedition. The Honor Guard's big event is the three-day Lewis and Clark Festival at Great Falls the third weekend in June. Contact Ron Ukrainetz, (406) 452-6041; e-mail cedrwing@mt.net

CAROL SCHOLL

The Brigade of Discovery, Washburn, North Dakota, gathers at the gates of the re-created Fort Mandan, where it depicts life at the winter quarters of the Lewis and Clark

Expedition in 1804-1805. Brigade members also portray North West Company and Hudson's Bay Company traders among the Mandan and Hidatsa Indians at that time. Contact Gary Anderson, Center, North Dakota, (701) 794-3628; e-mail vintagereproductions@westriv.com

KEN BOUC

Discovery Corps Inc. living historian Doug Kuony portrays the fiddle-playing Private George Gibson at Fort Atkinson State Historical Park. The Omaha-Council Bluffs-area group researches and re-creates daily life on the Lewis and Clark Expedition in 1804 as it passed through what are now Kansas, Iowa, Nebraska, and South Dakota. Discovery Corps conducts events on approximate dates and locations of actual Lewis and Clark rest and repair camps, reproducing for visitors the equipment, lifestyles and clothing of the explorers. A schedule is available online at: www.discoverycorps.org

KEN BOUC

Members of the **Frontier Army Living History Association, Fort Leavenworth, Kansas,** wear uniforms of an infantry first sergeant (left), a recruit, an infantry enlisted man and an artillery enlisted man. The association sponsors 12 men portraying soldiers of the Corps of Discovery uniformed and equipped as the Expedition was in the summer of 1804 when it was in the Fort Leavenworth vicinity. They appear in encampments, presentations and regularly scheduled events at the Frontier Army Museum at Fort Leavenworth. Contact the unit at (913) 684-3191/3767.

KEN BOUC

South Dakota Chapter, Lewis and Clark Trail Heritage Foundation's Bob Hanson of Yankton helps young Michael Morales of Yankton sign the camp register. The 40-member organization includes seven re-enactors, headed by Todd Wells of Brookings. The organization highlights South Dakota's role in the Lewis and Clark Expedition. Its re-enactors participate in events throughout South Dakota, but concentrate on encampments at Yankton, site of the Expedition's council with the Yankton Sioux, and Pierre, the site of the confrontation with the Teton Sioux. Contact Todd Wells at (605) 693-4440; fax (605) 697-8351.

KEN BOUC

Kids Learn History by Seeing and Doing

Gary Hemphill of Onawa, Iowa, explains use of a sextant to students on the banks of the Missouri River at Sunshine Bottoms in Boyd County, Nebraska. Hemphill and other living historians arrived on a replica of Lewis and Clark's white pirogue and demonstrated celestial navigation, early 19th century medicine, flintlock firearms and other features of the Expedition. The craft, built, by L & C Replicas and Butch Bouvier of Onawa, Iowa, was on its shakedown cruise.

24 Mayhew Cabin and Historic Village
Nebraska City, Nebraska. Formerly known as John Brown's Cave, this site sheltered runaway slaves. Open April through November. Admission charged. (402) 873-3115.

25 Schilling Wildlife Management Area
Northeast of Plattsmouth, Nebraska. Located at the confluence of the Platte and Missouri rivers, this largely undeveloped area is managed for waterfowl. Anglers, wildlife watchers and picnickers have access to a half mile of Platte River frontage and two miles of Missouri River frontage. Open April through October 14. NPGC. Free. (402) 296-0041. www.ngpc.state.ne.us/wildlife/schill.html

26 Fontenelle Forest
Bellevue, Nebraska. Spanning a Missouri River floodplain, this forested area boasts 17 miles of walking trails, including 1.3 miles of barrier-free boardwalk. It also includes a restored oxbow marsh, remains of 800-year-old American Indian lodges, an 1822 trading post and the Fred Buffett Forest Learning Center. Fontenelle Nature Association. Admission charged. (402) 731-3140. www.fontenelleforest.org

26 Durham Western Heritage Museum
Omaha, Nebraska. This converted railroad station has exhibits on the history of Omaha and the Union Pacific Railroad.Admission charged. (402) 444-5071. www.dwhm.org

26 Henry Doorly Zoo ■
Omaha, Nebraska. The Desert Dome, the newest addition at this world-class zoo and the world's largest glazed geodesic dome, allows visitors to see plants and animals from deserts around the world. Other exhibits include an indoor rain forest and a walk-through aquarium. Admission charged. (402) 733-8401. www.omahazoo.com

26 General Crook House Museum at Fort Omaha
Omaha, Nebraska. Located in the restored home of George Crook, a Civil War hero who later led campaigns against Indians, the collections at this living history museum include a Victorian garden and period furnishings. Historical Society of Douglas County. Admission charged. (402) 455-9990. www.omahahistory.org/museum.htm

The Desert Dome, a new attraction at the Henry Doorly Zoo in Omaha, is home to plants and animals from deserts around the world.

26 Joslyn Art Museum
Omaha, Nebraska. Omaha's premiere art museum has a remarkable collection of Western art, including the entire works of Swiss artist Karl Bodmer, whose watercolors and prints document his 1832-34 journey to the Missouri River frontier and show what the region probably looked like when the Lewis and Clark Expedition passed through. Admission charged. (402) 342-3300. www.joslyn.org

26 Lewis and Clark Landing
Omaha, Nebraska. Opening in late 2002, this park on the banks of the Missouri River will include a restaurant, boardwalk and a trail that will link it to other parks on the riverfront by 2004. A pedestrian bridge across the Missouri River, linking Omaha and Council Bluffs, is planned by 2005. Omaha Parks and Recreation. (402) 444-5900.

26 Neale Woods Nature Center
North edge of Omaha, Nebraska. Nine miles of trails lead visitors through native prairie, and hillside and floodplain forests along the Missouri River. Fontenelle Nature Association. Admission charged. (402) 453-5615. www.fontenelleforest.org

26 Mormon Trail Center at Historic Winter Quarters
Omaha, Nebraska. Visitors may explore a pioneer cabin, pull a handcart and see what life was like for thousands of Mormon pioneers who spent the winter of 1846-1847 here on their journey west. A nearby cemetery contains the graves of more than 500 people who died during the journey. Church of Jesus Christ of Latter Day Saints. Free. (402) 453-9372.

26 Lake Manawa State Park
Council Bluffs, Iowa. A natural Missouri River oxbow lake, Lake Manawa is a popular boating, fishing, swimming and camping spot. Trails connect with the Wabash Trace Trail, Council Bluffs Trail and the Western Historic Trails Center. IDNR. Free. (712) 366-0220. www.state.ia.us/dnr/organiza/ppd/manawa.htm

26 Rails West Railroad Museum
Council Bluffs, Iowa. Located in a restored Rock Island depot, the museum recalls the city's railroad history. (712) 323-5182.

26 Western Historic Trails Center
Council Bluffs, Iowa. This center tells the story of the Lewis and Clark Trail and the Oregon, California and Mormon pioneer trails. State Historical Society of Iowa. Free. (712) 366-4900. www.iowahistory.org/sites/western_trails/western_trails.html

26 Lewis & Clark Monument
North edge of Council Bluffs, Iowa. This bluff-top monument commemorates Lewis and Clark's visit to the area and their meeting with area American Indian tribes on Council Bluff, which eventually gave the city its name. The newly renovated monument overlooks the Missouri River Valley and the Omaha metro area.
(800) 228-6878.

26 Hitchcock Nature Area
Five miles north of Crescent, Iowa. Located in the loess hills, this area offers a nature center, primitive camping and 10 miles of hiking trails through woods and prairie. Pottawattamie County Conservation Board. Admission charged.
(712) 545-3283.
www.pottcoconservation.com/HNA.htm

27 Fort Atkinson State Historical Park ■
Fort Calhoun, Nebraska. Built in 1819 as the first U.S. military post west of the Missouri River, the fort is also near a bluff where Lewis and Clark held council with the Oto and Missouria Indians in 1804. Visitors may tour the reconstructed fort, an interpretive center and watch living-history demonstrations on select summer weekends. The park will host a Lewis and Clark national signature event from July 30 to August 3 in 2004. The grounds are open year-round and the visitor center is open weekdays from Memorial Day weekend through Labor Day and weekends from May through October. NGPC. Nebraska park entry permit required.
(402) 468-5611.
www.ngpc.state.ne.us/parks/showpark.ihtml?area_No=73

27 Boyer Chute National Wildlife Refuge
Three miles east of Fort Calhoun, Nebraska. The refuge features a two-mile long reconstructed chute that parallels the Missouri River. The area offers wildlife viewing, picnicking, nature trails, canoe launch and take-out sites, and fishing piers.
USFWS. Free.
(402) 468-4313.
http://midwest.fws.gov/desoto/boyerbro.html

27 Wilson Island Recreation Area
Four miles south and five miles west of Missouri Valley, Iowa. Located next to DeSoto National Wildlife Refuge, the area offers camping, picnicking and Missouri River access. IDNR. Free.
(712) 642-2069.
www.state.ia.us/government/dnr/organiza/ppd/wilsonis.htm

KEN BOUC

Old-time candy, treats and other items are available at the suttler's store at Fort Atkinson State Historical Park, located just north of Omaha in Fort Calhoun, Nebraska.

ERIC FOWLER

Badger Lake, located between Sloan and Whiting Iowa, is one of many oxbow lakes created when the Missouri River changed course. The lake is now a few miles from the river channel, which is visible at top left.

The Changed River

Lewis and Clark would not recognize most the Missouri River today. A third of the once-wild river remains in a natural or somewhat natural state. The remainder was forever changed as man attempted to tame the Big Muddy.

The river that the Corps of Discovery traveled up in 1804 and down in 1806 was dynamic and meandering. Throughout most its 2,400 miles, its channels, lined with sloughs and backwaters, were braided and full of snags, sandbars and islands. Each spring, runoff from rains and snowmelt would cause the river to rise. The deluge of water would resculpt the channel and change the river's course, leaving many oxbow lakes and marshes.

Even before man began to control the river in the early-1900s, its course had changed so dramatically that some of the places the Lewis and Clark Expedition had camped were under water or on the other side of the river.

The river's changing course was what drove man to control it. Each spring, farms, homes and even entire towns were swallowed by the shifting channel or flooded by rising water.

Taming of the Big Muddy began with the completion of Fort Peck Dam and Fort Peck Lake in Montana in 1938. Five more dams and reservoirs in North Dakota, South Dakota and Nebraska would follow, backing up water for a third of the river's length. The dams store the spring runoff, controlling floods and allowing the U.S. Army Corps of Engineers to meter water out for barge traffic in the lower third of river from Sioux City, Iowa, to St. Louis. That reach was channelized and straightened, shaving 72 miles off the river's length and creating more oxbows.

The changes have been good for man. With flooding no longer an annual event, more development, both agricultural and industrial, has occurred along the river. The dams generate hydroelectric power and the water pooled behind them creates boating, angling, camping and other recreational opportunities.

The cost was great to fish and wildlife, however. While reservoirs do provide habitat for some fish and wildlife, they now cover habitat once used by native fish and hundreds of thousands of acres of private and tribal land once productive as farm ground and pasture. The dams prevent species from moving up and downstream, and the changes in timing, duration and temperature of water released from dams serves as a detriment to both fish and wildlife in the reaches of the river between reservoirs and downstream. Channelization and the ensuing development erased a half-million acres of fish and wildlife habitat in the river's meander belt.

Recovery efforts are underway, but a decade-long battle on how to manage the river's flow continues to pit navigation, agriculture and other interests against the needs of fish and wildlife and the desire of upstream states to keep more water in reservoirs for recreation.

The only truly wild stretch of the Missouri River is found between the river's headwaters at Three Forks, Montana, and Fort Peck Reservoir and includes the Missouri National Wild and Scenic River. Unchannelized reaches between reservoirs, including 39 miles between Fort Randall Dam and Lewis and Clark Lake, and the 59-mile stretch between Gavins Point Dam and Ponca, Nebraska, also retain some natural characteristics.

These reaches make up the Missouri National Recreation River. At several access points and scenic overlooks, travelers can get a glimpse of the river and imagine what Lewis and Clark saw 200 years ago.

– Eric Fowler

27 DesoTo National Wildlife Refuge ■
Six miles west of Missouri Valley, Iowa. Displayed in the refuge visitor center are artifacts recovered in 1969 from the steamboat *Bertrand*, which sank on the Missouri River in 1865. The refuge's oxbow lake, created when the Missouri River was straightened, attracts tens of thousands of migrating snow geese in the fall. Deer, turkeys and other wildlife are abundant in the refuge's floodplain forest, marshes, crop fields and grasslands. The refuge also offers an auto tour, hiking trails, picnicking, boating and fishing. USFWS. Admission charged.
(712) 642-4121.
http:// midwest.fws.gov/desoto/dsotobro.html

28 Loess Hills State Forest
Four units located between Mondamin and Moorhead, Iowa. Forest and prairie in four locations in the loess hills includes Preparation Canyon State Park. IDNR. Free. (712) 456-2924.
www.state.ia.us/dnr/organiza/forest/lhsf.htm

29 Lewis and Clark State Park ■
Five miles west of Onawa, Iowa. Located on Blue Lake, visitors to this park can climb aboard a replica of the keelboat and pirogues used by the Corps of Discovery. The boats are on display in Blue Lake, a natural Missouri River oxbow lake, from April through October and will be displayed in the Lewis and Clark Visitor Center, which is scheduled for completion in fall of 2003, for the remainder of the year. The park offers campsites, trails, fishing, boating and swimming. IDNR. Free. (712) 423-2829.
www.state.ia.us/government/dnr/organiza/ppd/lewisclk.htm

29 Blackbird Scenic Overlook
North of Decatur, Nebraska. Located along U.S. Highway 75 near Blackbird Hill. On their way upriver in 1804, Lewis and Clark climbed the hill and left a flag on the grave of Omaha Chief Blackbird. A shelter modeled after an Omaha Indian earthlodge includes interpretive displays.

ERIC FOWLER

Diane Rollefson of Kingsley, Iowa, helps her sons, Zach and Austin, down from the upper deck of the replica keelboat on display at Lewis and Clark State Park near Onawa, Iowa.

30 Scenic Park
South Sioux City, Nebraska. This Missouri River park offers camping, picnicking, a walking path, fishing and more. Sioux City Parks and Recreation. (402) 494-7531

30 Chris Larsen Park
Sioux City, Iowa. This riverside park has a children's playground, outdoor entertainment center, sand volleyball courts, sculptures and a paved hike-bike trail that follows the Missouri and Big Sioux rivers. Free. (712) 279-6126.

30 Sergeant Floyd River Museum and Iowa/Nebraska Welcome Center
Sioux City, Iowa. Housed in a dry-docked survey boat on the banks of the Missouri River, the museum includes photos, dioramas and artifacts that detail the history of Missouri River transportation and Lewis and Clark exhibits. (712) 279-0198.

30 Sioux City Lewis and Clark Interpretive Center
Sioux City, Iowa. Scheduled to open in September 2002, this brand-new center will focus on the lesser-known members of the Expedition and give visitors an idea what it was like to be a

MICHAEL WYHE

Silverware and china are some of the artifacts recovered from the steamboat *Bertrand*, which sank in the Missouri River in 1865. The boat's recovered cargo is displayed at DeSoto National Wildlife Refuge near Missouri Valley, Iowa.

ERIC FOWLER

Floodlights illuminate the Sergeant Floyd Monument in Sioux City, Iowa, erected in honor of the only member of the Corps of Discovery to perish on the Expedition.

soldier serving under Lewis and Clark through interactive, hands-on displays. The center will retrace the explorers' route between Council Bluffs, Iowa, and Yankton, South Dakota, and focus on the science and medicine they used, the discoveries they made, the effects of the journey and the death of Sergeant Floyd. Free. (712) 224-5242. Sclcic@willinet.net

30 Sergeant Charles Floyd Monument and Park ■

Sioux City, Iowa. A 100-foot tall, white stone obelisk stands atop a bluff overlooking the Missouri where Sergeant Charles Floyd, the only man on the Lewis and Clark Expedition to die on the trip, was buried in 1804. A National Historic Landmark. Free.

30 Stone State Park

Northwestern edge of Sioux City, Iowa. Located in the loess hills overlooking the Big Sioux River, this scenic park features 20 miles of hiking, biking and horse trails, camping, fishing and scenic overlooks of three states. IDNR. Free. (712) 255-4698 www.state.ia.us/government/dnr/organiza/ppd/stone.htm

30 Dorothy Pecaut Nature Center

Northwestern edge of Sioux City, Iowa. Located within Stone State Park, this center depicts the region's prairie life, flora and fauna through exhibits and hands-on activities. Woodbury County Conservation Board. (712) 258-0838. www.woodburyparks.com/center.htm

Nebraska and South Dakota

30 Adams Homestead and Nature Preserve

West of North Sioux City, South Dakota. Visitors to this area, which includes Missouri River frontage and an oxbow lake, can explore more than eight miles of trails. Interpretive displays and picnicking are available. South Dakota Department of Game, Fish and Parks (SDGFP). Free. (605) 232-0873. www.state.sd.us/gfp/sdparks/adams/adams.htm

31 Ponca State Park ■

Two miles north of Ponca, Nebraska. Visitors to this scenic park can take a naturalist-led hayrack ride through grasslands, marshes and floodplain forest along the eastern end of the Missouri National Recreation River. They will be able to learn more about this 59-mile section of unchannelized river at the Missouri National Recreational River Resource and Education Center, tentatively set to open in July 2003. The park, located in the wooded hills above the river, also offers camping, cabins, trail rides, hayrack rides and a swimming pool. NGPC. Nebraska park entry permit required. (402) 755-2284. www.ngpc.state.ne.us/parks/showpark.ihtml?area_No=143

31 Missouri National Recreational River ■

Fort Randall Dam near Pickstown, South Dakota to Niobrara, Nebraska; and Gavins Point Dam near Yankton, South Dakota, to Ponca, Nebraska. Thirty-nine and 59 miles in length, respectively, these free-flowing stretches of the Missouri River, with islands, bars, chutes and snags, still exhibit the dynamic characteristics encountered by Lewis and Clark. Relatively undeveloped and with spectacular scenery, these reaches offer boating, fishing, canoeing, and camping, and include several state parks and recreation areas. There are also several landmarks identified by

ERIC FOWLER

Mike Malloy of Emerson, Nebraska, and Frank Baumert of Albion, Nebraska, canoe on the Missouri National Recreation River near Verdel, Nebraska.

Lewis and Clark. National Park Service. Access may require Nebraska or South Dakota park entry permit. (402) 667-5530. www.nps.gov/mnrr

31 Elk Point, South Dakota

In the first election west of the Mississippi, Patrick Gass was promoted to sergeant, filling a vacancy left by Sergeant Floyd's death. A marker retells the story and an annual festival commemorates the event.

32 W.H. Over Museum

Vermillion, South Dakota. Located on the University of South Dakota campus, the museum's Lewis & Clark – Spirit Mound Learning and Information Center includes a copy of Patrick Gass's journal, and a copy of Volume II of Lewis and Clark's journal, published in 1814. The museum also holds a collection of Sioux Indian artifacts and tells the story of the state's history, including westward expansion and Missouri River history. Free. (605) 677-5228. www.usd.edu/whover

32 Spirit Mound Historic Prairie

Six miles north of Vermillion, South Dakota. Lewis and Clark visited this site after being told they would find 18-inch tall devils. They found an open prairie described in the journals as a "most butifull landscape." That prairie is being restored today. A parking area has been constructed nearby and a hiking trail and picnicking area will be completed by 2003. Interpretive signs will be installed by 2004. (SDGFP). Free. (605) 987-2263. www.state.sd.us/gfp/sdparks/spiritmound/spiritmound.htm

32 Mulberry Bend Overlook

South of Vermillion, South Dakota. Located on the Nebraska side of a new bridge over the Missouri River, the overlook is on a wooded bluff more than 200 feet above the river and Mulberry Bend. Next to Nebraska Highway 15, the overlook is now open but won't be completed until interpretive panels are installed in early-2003. National Park Service. Free. (402) 336-3970.

ERIC FOWLER

31

Hayrack rides at Ponca State Park near Ponca, Nebraska, give visitors a close look at grasslands, marshes and cottonwood forests along an unchannelized stretch of the Missouri River.

33 Corps of Discovery Welcome Center

Three miles south of Yankton, South Dakota. Located at a scenic overlook, the center includes Lewis and Clark and other tourist information. (402) 667-6557.

33 Gavins Point National Fish Hatchery and Aquarium

Three miles west of Yankton, South Dakota. One of 70 federal hatcheries in the country, the hatchery raises a variety of fish, including the endangered pallid sturgeon. Located below Lewis and Clark Lake, the aquariums display 30 or more species of fish. The hatchery is open year-round, and the aquarium from May 1 to September 30. Nominal admission charged. (605) 665-3352. http://mountain-prairie.fws.gov/gavinspoint

33 Lewis and Clark Visitor Center

Ten miles north of Crofton, Nebraska. Located at Gavins Point Dam on Calumet Bluff, where Lewis and Clark met with the Yankton Sioux, this visitor center includes exhibits that detail the history of the Missouri River, including Lewis and Clark's journey. Tours of the nearby power plant are offered daily from Memorial Day through Labor Day. U.S. Army Corps of Engineers. Free. (402) 667-2546. www.nwo.usace.army.mil/html/Lake_Proj/gavinspoint/visit.html

33 **Lewis and Clark Lake**

Four miles west of Yankton, South Dakota. Formed by Gavins Point Dam, the southernmost of six dams on the Missouri River, this large, scenic reservoir is home to Nebraska and South Dakota recreation areas, some highly developed and some that are more primitive and secluded. U.S. Army Corps of Engineers. (402) 667-2546. www.nwo.usace.army.mil/html/Lake_Proj/gavinspoint/welcome.html

33 **Weigand-Burbach Area, Lewis and Clark State Recreation Area**

Nine miles north and five west of Crofton, Nebraska. This modern park includes a marina, cabins, camping, picnicking, swimming, boating and fishing on the south shore of Lewis and Clark Lake. NGPC. Nebraska park entry permit required. (402) 388-4169. www.ngpc.state.ne.us/parks/showpark.ihtml?area_No=101

33 **Lewis and Clark Recreation Area**

Four miles west of Yankton, South Dakota. This modern resort offers a marina, boating, cabins, camping, fishing, playgrounds, picnicking, swimming and more. SDGFP. South Dakota park entrance license is required. (605) 668-2985. www.state.sd.us/gfp/sdparks/lewis/lewis.htm

34 **Chief Standing Bear Memorial Bridge Turnout**

East of Niobrara, Nebraska. Located on the South Dakota side of the Missouri River along South Dakota Highway 37, the overlook gives visitors a high vantage point from which to view the river. Interpretive signs tell the story of Standing Bear, whose plight led to a U.S. District Court decision in 1879 that for the first time recognized American Indians as people under the law. National Park Service. Free. (402) 336-3970.

34 **Niobrara State Park**

Five miles west of Niobrara, Nebraska. Visitors to this park may tour the Missouri National Recreation River on a Zodiac raft and get a view of what Lewis and Clark saw. Overlooking the confluence of the Niobrara and Missouri rivers, this scenic park offers cabins, camping, hiking and horse trails and a swimming pool. NGPC. Nebraska park entry permit required. (402) 857-3373. www.ngpc.state.ne.us/parks/showpark.ihtml?area_No=126

34 **The George Shannon Trail**

A dozen northeastern Nebraska communities are promoting this trail to honor Shannon, the youngest member of the Expedition who became lost for 16 days in the area. Wooden statues of Shannon, carved by a local chainsaw artist, will be displayed at businesses in Bloomfield, Center, Creighton, Crofton, Lindy, Niobrara, Verdigre, Winnetoon, Wausa, the Wynot area (St. Helena, St. James, Bow Valley and Wynot), Hartington and Santee. www.shannontrail.cjb.net

35 **Old Baldy** ■

Six miles north of Lynch, Nebraska. It was at this cone-shaped landmark overlooking the Missouri River where Lewis and Clark captured the first prairie dog. An interpretive sign is planned for a turnout that has been built on a county road near Old Baldy, which is also known as The Tower.

KEN BOUC

Old Baldy, or "the Cupola" in journals of Lewis and Clark, overlooks the Missouri River north of Lynch, Nebraska.

South Dakota

36 **Lake Francis Case**

Pickstown, South Dakota. Formed by Fort Randall Dam, the lake stretches 107 miles. Twenty-two state and federal recreation areas offer camping, boating, fishing, picnicking and other activities along the lake. U.S. Army Corps of Engineers. (605) 487-7845. www.nwo.usace.army.mil/html/Lake_Proj/fortrandall/welcome.html

37 **Lewis and Clark Information Center**

Chamberlain, South Dakota. From a bluff overlooking the Missouri River, this center tells about Lewis and Clark's adventures in South Dakota. Included in the displays are a stylized keelboat, trade goods and supplies taken on the voyage. Other exhibits include information on the American Indian tribes the explorers met and the wildlife they discovered. Currently

KEN BOUC

A diorama of a Lakota family and lodge is one of several American Indian exhibits at the Akta Lakota Museum at the St. Joseph's Indian School in Chamberlain, South Dakota.

open mid-May through October. South Dakota Department of Tourism. Free. (605) 734-4562.

37 Akta Lakota Museum ■

Chamberlain, South Dakota. Visitors learn about the rich culture of the Teton Sioux through exhibits that include authentic Lakota beadwork and quillwork, ceremonial dress, traditional weaponry and tools, and a mounted buffalo. Part of the St. Joseph's Indian School, the museum strives to preserve and promote the Sioux Culture. Nearby, visitors can hike a prairie trail above the Missouri at Roam Free Park. Free. (605) 734-3452. www.stjo.org/museum/index.htm

37 Native American Scenic Byway

Chamberlain, South Dakota. This scenic drive follows the Missouri River from Chamberlain to Pierre through the Crow Creek and Lower Brule Indian reservations. It passes over grassy hills and bluffs above the river and through the woodlands and wetlands along it. Along the way, travelers can see various wildlife, including tribal herds of buffalo. Guides are available at the Circle of Tepees Information Center in Oacoma. (605) 473-0561. www.byways.org/travel/byway.html?CX_BYWAY=1046

38 Lake Sharpe ■

Fort Thompson, South Dakota. Formed by Big Bend Dam, the lake offers camping, boating, fishing, picnicking and other activities at 24 state and federal recreation areas. The lake covers the feature of the Missouri River noted by Lewis and Clark that gave the dam its name – a 25-mile long bend that takes the river nearly in a full circle before returning to a spot where the land separating the river from itself is only a mile wide. U.S. Army Corps of Engineers. (605) 245-2255. www.nwo.usace.army.mil/html/Lake_Proj/bigbend/welcome.html

39 Fort Pierre National Grassland

Five miles south of Fort Pierre, South Dakota. Visitors can experience the wide-open Great Plains and see rolling hills and prairie that looks much as it did when Lewis and Clark visited. The area covers 180 square miles,

SOUTH DAKOTA TOURISM

Lake Sharpe near Fort Thompson is one of six reservoirs on the Missouri River, including four in South Dakota, that draw anglers nationwide.

SOUTH DAKOTA TOURISM

40 A bicyclist stops at a replica Arikara lodge at West Whitlock Recreation Area at Lake Oahe near Gettysburg, South Dakota.

Indian Tribes

Eleven American Indian tribes live along the Lewis and Clark trail between St. Louis and Washburn, North Dakota. Some lived on the Missouri River when Lewis and Clark came upriver in 1804. Others were moved onto reservations along the river by the United States as Euroamericans settled in the West.

The tribes have rich histories, and most hold annual pow wows to celebrate their heritage. The following are telephone numbers to reach the tribes for more information.

Iowa
White Cloud, Kansas
(913) 595-3258

Sac and Fox
Reserve, Kansas
(913) 742-7471

Omaha
Macy, Nebraska
(402) 329-6774

Winnebago
Winnebago, Nebraska
(402) 878-2272

Yankton Sioux
Marty, South Dakota
(605) 384-5687

Santee Sioux
Santee, Nebraska.
(402) 857-2302.

Ponca
Niobrara, Nebraska
(402) 857-3391

Crow Creek Sioux
Fort Thompson, South Dakota
(605) 245-2221

Lower Brule Sioux
Lower Brule, South Dakota
(605) 473-5561

Cheyenne River Sioux
Eagle Butte, South Dakota
(605) 964-4155

Standing Rock Sioux
Fort Yates, North Dakota
(701) 854-7207

intermingled with private rangeland and cropland. Mule and white-tailed deer, pronghorns, prairie dogs and prairie grouse live on the grassland. USDA Forest Service. Free. (605) 224-5517. www.fs.fed.us/r2/nebraska/units/fp/ftpierre.html

39 Lilly Park

Fort Pierre, South Dakota. This small park includes the mouth of the Bad River, the site of a tense meeting between Lewis and Clark and the Teton Sioux. Free.

39 The Verendrye Monument

Fort Pierre, South Dakota. In 1913, high school students unearthed a lead tablet that was placed on this hill overlooking the Missouri River Valley in 1743 by French Canadian explorers and brothers, Chevalier and Louis La Verendrye, claiming the land for France. A monument marks the spot, now a National Historic Landmark. The tablet is on display in Pierre's South Dakota Cultural Heritage Center. www.fortpierre.com/vm.html

39 Lake Oahe

Pierre, South Dakota. Formed by Oahe Dam, the lake includes 2,250 miles of shoreline stretching into North Dakota. Fifty-one state and federal recreation areas around the lake offer camping, boating, fishing, picnicking and other activities. The Oahe Dam Visitor Center highlights the construction of the dam, the Lewis and Clark Expedition and the fish of South Dakota. U.S. Army Corps of Engineers. (605) 224-5862. www.nwo.usace.army.mil/html/Lake_Proj/oahe/welcome.html

39 Cultural Heritage Center

Pierre, South Dakota. The museum showcases Sioux Indian life and culture and the pioneer, political and military history of the state. It also includes a replica of the Jefferson Peace and Friendship Medal, which Lewis and Clark presented to tribes they met, and an exhibit that details the explorers' journey through what would become South Dakota. Admission charged. (605) 773-3458.

40 West Whitlock Recreation Area ■

Fifteen miles west of Gettysburg, South Dakota. Lewis and Clark spent several days in an Arikara Indian village in 1804. This state recreation area on Lake Oahe includes a replica of an Arikara lodge made with cottonwood logs, willow branches and grass, as well as an interpretive center, hiking trails, cabins, camping, swimming, picnicking, fishing, boating and more. SDGFP. South Dakota park entry license required. (605) 765-9410. www.state.sd.us/gfp/sdparks/whitlock/whitlock.htm

41 Monument to Sacagawea

Six miles west and four south of Mobridge, South Dakota. The only woman to join the Corps of Discovery,

Sacagawea died at nearby Fort Manuel six years after the Expedition was completed. A monument to her sits on a bluff overlooking Lake Oahe. Nearby is the gravesite of Sitting Bull. Contact Mobridge Chamber of Commerce. Free.
(605) 845-2387.

North Dakota

42 Sitting Bull Burial State Historic Site

Fort Yates, North Dakota. Located on the Standing Rock Sioux Indian Reservation is the original burial site of the great American Indian chief Sitting Bull.

43 Fort Abraham Lincoln State Park

Seven miles south of Mandan, North Dakota. Featured at this park are reconstructed Mandan Indian earthlodges of the On-A-Slant Indian village, the ruins of which were noted by Lewis and Clark. The Mandans lived at this site for more than 200 years and built a thriving trade center before a smallpox epidemic hit in 1781. Portions of Fort Abraham Lincoln, from which Lieutenant Colonel George Armstrong Custer and the Seventh Cavalry rode out on their ill-fated expedition against the Sioux at the Little Big Horn, have been reconstructed, including the Custer House. Located on the Missouri River, the park also offers a visitor center, camping, picnicking, boating, fishing, trails and more. North Dakota Parks and Recreation Department (NDPR). North Dakota park entry permit required. (701) 663-9571.
www.state.nd.us/ndparks/Parks/FLSP.htm

43 North Dakota Heritage Center

Bismarck, North Dakota. Located on the grounds of the state capitol, the museum features exhibits on North Dakota history, including dinosaurs, early American Indians, the Lewis and Clark Expedition, the Indian War period and the immigration of white settlers. At the entrance of the center is a statue honoring Sacagawea. State Historical Society of North Dakota. Free.
(701) 328-2666.
www.state.nd.us/hist/hcenter.htm

43 Lewis and Clark Riverboat ■

Bismarck, North Dakota. Dinner and sightseeing cruises on the scenic Missouri River are offered on this paddlewheel riverboat from Memorial Day through Labor Day and by charter from April through October. Fee charged. (701) 255-4233.
www.lewisandclarkriverboat.com

43 Double Ditch State Historic Site

Seven miles north of Bismarck. Deserted when Lewis and Clark passed, this Mandan earthlodge village was protected by two ditches. The remains of these ditches and earthlodges are visible today. State Historical Society of North Dakota. Free. (701) 328-2672.

44 Cross Ranch Centennial State Park

Eleven miles southeast of Hensler, North Dakota. Visitors here can rent a canoe and explore an unchannelized stretch of the Missouri. The park also offers the River Peoples Visitor Center, with displays on Missouri River history, camping, hiking, boating and picnicking. NDPR. North Dakota park entry permit required.
(701) 794-3731.
www.state.nd.us/ndparks/Parks/CRSP.htm

44 North Dakota Lewis & Clark Interpretive Center

Washburn, North Dakota. The center looks at the entire Lewis and Clark Expedition, with emphasis on the first winter spent at Fort Mandan. Displays include a wooden canoe carved from the trunk of a large cottonwood tree and other American Indian artifacts from most of the tribes the explorers met. The North Dakota Lewis & Clark Bicentennial Foundation. Admission charged.
(877) 462-8535.
www.fortmandan.com

44 Fort Mandan

Washburn, North Dakota. Built by members of the Lewis and Clark Expedition downriver from the Mandan and Hidatsa villages, the fort was named after the American Indians who greeted the explorers on October 25, 1804, and visited them often during the winter. The reconstructed fort is within a few miles of the original location. Interpreters are on site year-round. A new visitor center opened in 2002. North Dakota Lewis & Clark Bicentennial Foundation. Admission charged. (877) 462-8535.
www.fortmandan.com

Rides are available on the *Lewis and Clark Riverboat* on the Missouri River from Port of Bismarck in North Dakota.

Signature Events

Many special events and celebrations will be held along the Lewis and Clark trail during the 200th anniversary of the explorers' journey. Thirteen have been chosen as National Signature Events.

The events and the communities that host them were selected for their place in the Expedition's chronology, historical relevance, cultural diversity, tribal involvement, geographic location and sponsoring organizations' capacity. More signature events might be added. More information is available at www.lewisandclark200.org.

January 18, 2003, Charlottesville, Virginia
The home of President Thomas Jefferson, Monticello, will be the site of the first event.

October 24-26, 2003, Louisville, Kentucky, Clarksville, Indiana
At the Falls of the Ohio River, Clark and other members of the Expedition joined Lewis.

Spring, 2004, St. Louis and St. Charles, Missouri and Hartford and Wood River, Illinois
The Expedition left its first winter encampment at Camp River DuBois and headed up the Missouri River, making its first stop at St. Charles.

July 3-4, 2004, Atchison and Fort Leavenworth, Kansas, and Kansas City, Missouri
The Expedition camped three days at the confluence of the Kansas and Missouri rivers in what is now Kansas City, Kansas, and celebrated their first July 4th in the West near Independence Creek.

July 30-August 3, 2004, Omaha, Nebraska
The Expedition made first contact with American Indians north of present-day Omaha. Fort Atkinson, built on the site 20 years later and now a state historical park, will host some events.

August 27-September 26, 2004, Chamberlain, Oacoma and tribal lands in South Dakota
Lewis and Clark met with two tribes they called the Yankton Sioux and the Teton Sioux in what is now South Dakota. Members of the Dakota, Lakota and Nakota nations will tell of the historic encounters with the explorers and share their cultural values.

October 22-31, 2004, Bismarck, North Dakota
The Corps of Discovery was greeted with hospitality by the Mandan, Hidatsa and Arikara Indians. The explorers spent the winter of 1804-1805 near the Mandan and Hidatsa villages.

July 3-4, 2005, Great Falls, Montana
The explorers spend their second July 4th in the West at the Great Falls of the Missouri River.

Fall, 2005, lower Columbia River, Oregon and Washington
The explorers made it over the mountains, descended the rivers and finally reached their goal, the Pacific Ocean, November 7, 1805.

June 14-17, 2006, Clearwater River, Idaho
On their return trip, the explorers spent time with the Nez Perce Tribe on the Clearwater River as they waited for snowpack to recede in the Bitterroot Mountains.

July 25, 2006, Pompey's Pillar, Billings, Montana
On the return trip, Clark came down the Yellowstone River and inscribed his name in Pompey's Pillar, which he named in honor of Sacagawea's infant son, who he called "Pomp."

August 17-20, 2006, New Town, North Dakota
Historical Homelands of the Mandan, Hidatsa, and Arikara nations. Lewis and Clark returned to the Knife River Indian village and there parted company with Sacagawea, who will be the focus of this event.

September 22-24, 2006, St. Louis, Missouri
Thought by many to have perished after not returning a year earlier as planned, the explorers were greeted by a joyous reception as they ended their journey in St. Louis.

45 Fort Clark State Historic Site
Fort Clark, North Dakota. A fur trading post named in honor of William Clark and in service from 1830 to the 1850s, this was one of three major forts built on the Missouri River. It was also where a steamboat brought the smallpox virus that decimated neighboring Mandan, Hidatsa and Arikara Indian populations. Visitors may take a self-guided tour of the grounds and earthlodge remains. Open May 16 to September 15. Free. State Historical Society of North Dakota. (701) 328-2672 or (701) 794-8832.

45 Knife River Indian Villages National Historic Site ■
Stanton, North Dakota. Located above the confluence of the Knife and Missouri rivers, the site preserves the historical and archaeological remnants of the Hidatsa villages where Sacagawea, the woman who went west with Lewis and Clark, lived. The site includes a fully furnished Hidatsa earthlodge, visitor center, interpretive displays and 13 miles of hiking trails, including a self-guided walking tour. National Park Service. Free. (701) 745-3300. www.nps.gov/knri

CHUCK HANEY

A fully furnished Hidatsa earthlodge is one of many attractions at the Knife River Indian Villages National Historic Site at Stanton, North Dakota.

Acknowledgments

We gratefully acknowledge the following organizations and individuals for their support and assistance during the production of this publication:

The National Park Service, for partial funding under a National Park Service Challenge Cost Share Grant.

Gary E. Moulton and The University of Nebraska Press, for the use of information and quotations from: *Meriwether Lewis and William Clark, The Journals of the Lewis and Clark Expedition.* Edited by Gary E. Moulton, Lincoln, Nebraska: The University of Nebraska Press, 1983-2001.

The National Geographic Society and Vineyard Productions, for permission to photograph during the filming for the large-format film, *Lewis and Clark: Great Journey West,* on the Missouri River near Niobrara, Nebraska.

Archives and Illustration Sources

Independence National Historical Park, 313 Walnut Street, Philadelphia, PA 19106, www.nps.gov/inde/

Library of Congress, 101 Independence Ave., S.E., Washington, D.C. 29540 (202) 707-5000, www.loc.gov/

Missouri Historical Society, P.O. Box 11940, St. Louis, MO 63112-0040, (314) 746-4511, www.mohistory.org

Academy of Natural Sciences of Philadelphia, Ewell Sale Steward Library, 1900 Benjamin Franklin Parkway, Philadelphia, PA 19118, (215) 299-1000, www.acnastsci.org

Joslyn Art Museum, 2200 Dodge Street, Omaha, NE 68102-1292. (402) 342-3303, www.joslyn.org

Gary R. Lucy Gallery, 231 West Main St., Washington, MO 63090, (636) 239-6337, www.garylucy.com

Michael Haynes Historic Art, 19050 Fox Run Hollow, Wildwood, Missouri 63069, www.michaelhaynesart.com

Louis Archambault Limited Edition Prints, 331 West Lawrence, Helena, MT 59601, (406) 443-8206, members.aol.com/injwif

Missouri Conservation Heritage Foundation, P.O. Box 366, Jefferson City, MO, (573) 634-2080

Beinecke Rare Book and Manuscript Library, Yale collection of Western Americana, Yale University, 121 Wall Street, New Haven, CT 06510, www.library.yale.edu/beinecke/blgwa.htm

The Fort Leavenworth Historical Society, 100 Reynolds Avenue, Fort Leavenworth, KS 66027-2334, (913) 651-7400

Smithsonian American Art Museum, 750 Ninth Street, N.W., Suite 3100, Washington, D.C. 20001-4505 (202) 275-1500, www.nmaa.si.edu/

Gilcrease Museum, 1400 Gilcrease Museum Road, Tulsa, OK 74127, (918 596-2705, www.gilcrease.org

Lewis & Clark Trail Maps: Cartographic Reconstruction, Volume I by Martin Plamondon II by permission from Washington State University, Office of University Publications and Printing, P.O. Box 645910, Pullman, WA 99164-5910, www.wsu.edu/wsupress

Charles Fritz Publishing, 8912 Susanna Drive, Billings, MT 59101, (225) 767-3183, www.charlesfritz.com

The American Philosophical Society Library, 105 South Fifth Street, Philadelphia, PA 19106-3386, (215) 440-3400, www.amphilsoc.org

National Museum of Wildlife Art, 2820 Rungus Road, Jackson Hole, WY 83001, (307) 733-5771, www.wildlifeart.org

Montana Historical Society, 225 North Roberts, Helena, MT 59620-1201. (406) 444-2694, www.montanahistoricalsociety.org

Diamond L Bar Studios, Ron Ukrainetz, 2104 5th Avenue South, Great Falls, MT 59405. (406) 452-6041, www.RonUkrainetz.com

Clymer Museum of Art, Mrs. John F. Clymer, 416 North Pearl, Ellensburg, WA 98926, (509) 962-6416, www.clymermuseum.com

Idaho Forest Industries, Hayden, Idaho.

Headwaters Chapter, Lewis and Clark Trail Heritage Foundation, Box 577, Bozeman, MT 59771

Artwork and Artifact Credits

America Looks West – Contents, pages 2-7
3: Lewis and Clark portraits, Charles Willson Peale, Independence National Historical Park; Nicholas King map, Library of Congress. 4-5: David Schultz photo, Missouri Historical Society.

Poised for Discovery, pages 8-13
9: Charles Willson Peale, Independence National Historical Park. 10: Frederick Pursh, Academy of Natural Sciences of Philadelphia. 10-11: Karl Bodmer, Joslyn Art Museum. 12-13: Karl Bodmer, Joslyn Art Museum.

A Corps of Discovery, pages 14-31
14-15: Gary R. Lucy, Gary R. Lucy Gallery; 16: Louis Archambault, Louis Archambault Limited Edition Prints. 16-17: Mark S. Raithel, Missouri Conservation Heritage Foundation. 18: Glenn S. Hensley photo, Missouri Historical Society. 19: Michael Haynes, Michael Haynes Historic Art. 20: Michael Haynes, Michael Haynes Historic Art. 21: Bob Little, Allied Photocolor photo, Missouri Historical Society. 22-23: Karl Bodmer, Joslyn Art Museum. 24: Glenn S. Hensley photo, Missouri Historical Society. 25: Michael Haynes, Michael Haynes Historic Art. 26-27: Karl Bodmer, Joslyn Art Museum. 27: Clark journal entry January 21, 1804, Beinecke Rare Book and Manuscript Library. 28-29: Rick Reeves, The Fort Leavenworth Historical Society.

The Plains Commence, pages 32-49
32-33: George Catlin, Smithsonian American Art Museum. 34: George Catlin, Gilcrease Museum. 35: Martin Plamondon II, Washington State University Press. 36: Michael Haynes, Michael Haynes Historic Art. 37: Philip Reinagle, Beinecke Rare Book and Manuscript Library 38: John James Audubon, Academy of Natural Sciences of Philadelphia. 39: John James Audubon, Academy of Natural Sciences of Philadelphia. 40: Ken Bouc, Frontier Army Living History Association, Fort Leavenworth. 40-41: Michael Haynes, Michael Haynes Historic Art. 42: Karl Bodmer, Joslyn Art Museum 43: Ken Bouc, Frontier Army Living History Association, Fort Leavenworth. 44-45: Charles Fritz, Charles Fritz Publishing. 45: Titian Ramsay Peale, Academy of Natural Sciences of Philadelphia. 46: Ken Bouc, South Dakota Chapter of the Lewis and Clark Trail Heritage Foundation. 47: Karl Bodmer, Joslyn Art Museum. 48: Ken Bouc, Frontier Army Living History Association, Fort Leavenworth. 49: Karl Bodmer, Joslyn Art Museum.

Land of the Short Grass, pages 50-65
51: Michael Haynes, Michael Haynes Historic Art. 52: Titian Ramsay Peale, American Philosophical Society Library. 53: Karl Bodmer, Joslyn Art Museum. 54: William Jacob Hays, National Museum of Wildlife Art. 55: Titian Ramsay Peale, American Philosophical Society Library. 56 (bottom, left): Clark journal entry February 5, 1805, American Philosophical Society Library. 56 (top, right): Karl Bodmer, Joslyn Art Museum. 58: Charles Fritz, Charles Fritz Publishing. 59: George Catlin, Gilcrease Museum. 60-61: Charles Russell, Montana Historical Society. 62-63: Karl Bodmer, Joslyn Art Museum. 64-65: Charles Fritz, Charles Fritz Publishing.

Moulton's Journal, pages 66-71
66-67: Michael Haynes, Michael Haynes Historic Art. 68: American Philosophical Society Library. 69 (top): Clark journal entry February 1, 1806, American Philosophical Society Library. 70: Clark journal entry February 16, 1806, American Philosophical Society Library. 71 (top): Lewis journal entry March 15, 1806, American Philosophical Society Library. 71 (bottom): Lewis journal entry, March 16, 1806, American Philosophical Society Library.

Stepping Off the Map, pages 72-91
72-73: Charles Fritz, Charles Fritz Publishing. 74: Clark journal entry, July 4, 1805, American Philosophical Society Library; 74-75: Ron Ukrainetz, Diamond L Bar Studios. 76-77: John F. Clymer, Clymer Museum of Art. 78-79: Charles Russell, Idaho Forest Industries, Hayden, Idaho. 80-81: Charles Russell, Montana Historical Society. 82-83: John F. Clymer, Clymer Museum of Art. 83: Louis Archambault, Louis Archambault Limited Edition Prints. 84: Frederick Pursh, American Philosophical Society Library. 84-85: John F. Clymer, Clymer Museum of Art. 86: Frederick Pursh, American Philosophical Society Library. 87: John F. Clymer, Clymer Museum of Art. 88: Alexander Wilson, Academy of Natural Sciences of Philadelphia. 88-89: John F. Clymer, Clymer Museum of Art 90-91: Robert F. Morgan, Headwaters Chapter, Lewis and Clark Trail Heritage Foundation.

The Expedition Endures, pages 94-99
94 (bottom): Charles Willson Peale, American Philosophical Society Library. 94-95: Nicholas King map, Library of Congress. 96-97: Samuel Lewis map, Library of Congress. 98: Lewis journal cover, American Philosophical Society. 99: Karl Bodmer, Joslyn Art Museum.

The Tribes: "We Have Survived", pages 100-103
101: Karl Bodmer, Joslyn Art Museum. 102 (top): Karl Bodmer, Joslyn Art Museum. 102 (bottom): Karl Bodmer, Joslyn Art Museum. 103: Karl Bodmer, Joslyn Art Museum

Traveling with Lewis and Clark, pages 104-128
109: Allied Photocolor, Missouri Historical Society.

America Looks West

Lewis and Clark on the Missouri

Coordinator: *Ken Bouc*
Editors: *Tom White, Doug Carroll*
Principal Writers: *Harry W. Fritz, Bob Moore, Jay H. Buckley, Ken Bouc, Ken Rogers, Robert C. Carriker, Gerard Baker, Eric Fowler*
Contributing Writers: *Hal Stearns, Terry Fingerhut, Steven Allie*
Art Director: *Tim Reigert*

NEBRASKALAND MAGAZINE STAFF

Editor: Tom White
Associate Editor: Doug Carroll
Art Director: Tim Reigert
Senior Editors: Ken Bouc, Jon Farrar
Regional Editors: Bob Grier, Rocky Hoffmann, Eric Fowler
Contributing Editors: Michael Forsberg, Tom Keith
Circulation: Donna Robinson
Photo Librarian: Terry Fingerhut

NEBRASKA GAME AND PARKS COMMISSION

Administration
Director: Rex Amack
Assistant Directors: Noelyn Isom, Roger Kuhn, Kirk Nelson
Information and Education Administrator: Paul Horton
Information and Education Art Director: Steve O'Hare

Board of Commissioners
Chairman: John P. Miller, Blair
Vice Chairman: Connie Lapaseotes, Bridgeport
2nd Vice Chairman: Randall K. Stinnette, Inland

Marvin Westcott, Holdrege
James Stuart Jr., Lincoln
Bill Grewcock, Omaha
Rob Coupland, Valentine

Inside Back Cover: Straining on the oars in the fading light of late-summer, crewmen pull a replica keelboat past Missouri River bluffs near Niobrara during the filming of *Lewis and Clark: Great Journey West,* a large-format film. Photo by Eric Fowler.

NEBRASKAland Magazine
Published by the Nebraska Game and Parks Commission